The
Boston
Terrier

An Owner's Guide To

A HAPPY HEALTHY PET

Howell Book House

IDG Books Worldwide, Inc.
An International Data Group Company
Foster City, CA • Chicago, IL • Indianapolis, IN • New York, NY

Howell Book House
IDG Books Worldwide, Inc.
An International Data Group Company
919 E. Hillsdale Boulevard,
Suite 400
Foster City, CA 94404

For general information on IDG Books Worldwide's books in the U.S., please call our
Consumer Customer Service department at 800-762-2974. For reseller information,
including discounts and premium sales, please call our Reseller Customer Service
department at 800-434-3422.

Library of Congress Cataloging-in-Publication Data
Meade, Scottee.
The Boston terrier/[Scottee Meade].
p. cm.—(An owner's guide to a happy healthy pet)
Includes bibliographical references (p.).
ISBN 1-58245-159-1
1. Boston Terrier   I. Howell Book House. II. Series
SF429.B7M33   2000   00-038475
636'.72—dc21   CIP

Manufactured in the United States of America
10 9 8 7 6 5 4 3 2 1

Series Director: Susanna Thomas
Book Design by Michele Laseau
Cover Design by Iris Jeromnimon
External Features Illustration by Shelley Norris
Other Illustrations by Jeff Yesh
Photography:
  Front and back cover by Jeannie Harrison
  All photography by Mary Bloom unless otherwise noted.
    Joan Balzarini: 96
    Mary Bloom: 96, 136, 145
    Paulette Braun/Pets by Paulette: 96
    Buckinghambill American Cocker Spaniels: 148
    Sian Cox: 134
    Dr. Ian Dunbar: 98, 101, 103, 111, 116–117, 122, 123, 127
    Dan Lyons: 96
    Cathy Merrithew: 129
    Liz Palika: 133
    Susan Rezy: 96–97
    Judith Strom: 96, 107, 110, 128, 130, 135, 137, 139, 140, 144, 149, 150
Production Team: Heather Gregory, Angel Perez, and Heather Pope

Contents

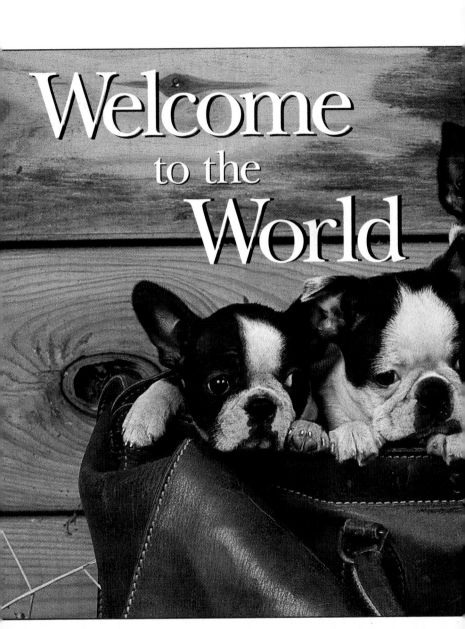

Welcome
to the
World

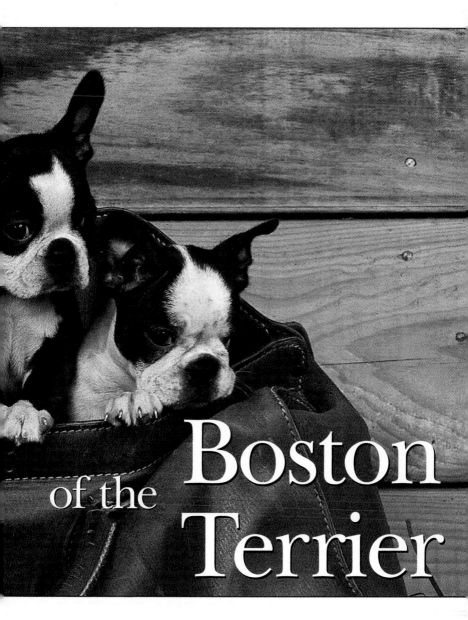

of the Boston Terrier

External Features of the Boston Terrier

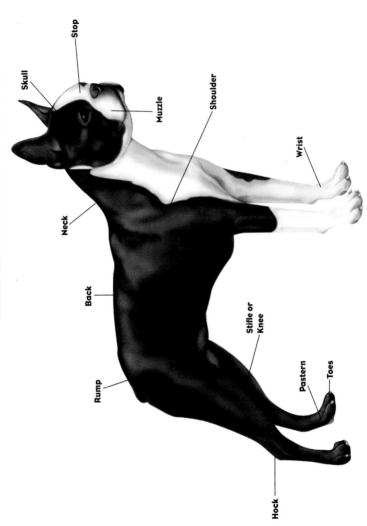

chapter 1

What Is a Boston Terrier?

The Boston Terrier is one of the earliest breeds developed in the United States to be recognized by the American Kennel Club (AKC). The breed was developed in Boston, Massachusetts, in the middle of the nineteenth century. Despite its name, the Boston Terrier is classified by the AKC in the Non-Sporting Group, not the Terrier Group. Part of the breed's ancestry does

include certain terriers, but Bostons have not been bred for the traditional terrier tasks of hunting or fighting.

The Boston earned the nickname "The American Gentleman" because of its origin, its markings suggestive of formal attire and its

5

refined temperament. The breed was recognized early in its development as an outstanding companion dog. In selecting a Boston to share your life, you are choosing a dog whose ancestors have graced the hearths of American homes for more than a century. Bostons sport a low-maintenance coat, a friendly, easygoing temperament and a size that makes them, in a word, portable.

The standard of perfection for the breed, written by the Boston Terrier Club of America and accepted by the AKC, details the physical characteristics that define this unique breed. Understanding the standard will enable you to select a sound, healthy dog that will be a wonderful companion for you and your family.

THE AMERICAN KENNEL CLUB

Familiarly referred to as "the AKC," the American Kennel Club is a nonprofit organization devoted to the advancement of purebred dogs. The AKC maintains a registry of recognized breeds, and it adopts and enforces rules for dog events, such as shows, obedience trials, field trials, hunting tests, lure coursing, herding, earthdog trials, agility and the Canine Good Citizen program.

The AKC is a club of clubs, established in 1884 and composed, today, of over 500 autonomous dog clubs throughout the United States. Each club is represented by a delegate; the delegates make up the legislative body of the AKC, voting on rules and electing directors.

The AKC maintains the *Stud Book*—the record of every dog ever registered with the AKC. It also publishes a variety of materials on purebred dogs, including a monthly magazine, books and numerous educational pamphlets. For more information, contact the AKC at the address listed at the end of this chapter or in Chapter 13, "Resources." For the names of AKC publications, look in Chapter 12, "Recommended Reading."

General Appearance

The Boston Terrier is a lively, highly intelligent, smoothcoated, short headed, compactly built, short-tailed, well balanced dog, brindle, seal or black in color and evenly marked with white. The head is in proportion to the size of the dog and the expression indicates a high degree of intelligence.

The body is rather short and well knit, the limbs strong and neatly turned, the tail is short and no feature is so prominent that the dog appears badly proportioned. The dog conveys an impression of determination, strength and activity, with style of a high order; carriage easy and graceful. A proportionate combination of "Color and White Markings" is a particularly distinctive feature of a representative specimen.

The first two paragraphs give a clear, overall description of the Boston: lively, intelligent, compact, smooth-coated. The Boston is a square, well-proportioned animal. Its unique head shape is a distinctive feature of the breed, but the head must be in proper proportion to the other features of the body.

SIZE, PROPORTION, SUBSTANCE

Weight is divided by classes as follows: Under 15 pounds; 15 pounds and under 20 pounds; 20 pounds and not to exceed 25 pounds. The length of leg must balance with the length of body to give the Boston Terrier its striking square appearance. The Boston Terrier is a sturdy dog and must not appear to be either spindly or coarse. The bone and muscle must be in proportion as well as an enhancement to the dog's weight and structure. Fault: Blocky or chunky in appearance.

The standard provides for a relatively broad range of size within the breed. There is no minimum weight, although few Bostons weigh less than 10 pounds full grown. The maximum weight listed is 25 pounds. Although some Bostons do grow larger than 25 pounds, dogs of that size tend to lose some of the characteristics that define the breed, including compactness. Many people have a definite preference for a particular size of Boston. One person may seek a smaller dog of 12 to 15 pounds; others love the larger specimens of 20 to 25 pounds.

According to the AKC standard, the Boston Terrier is an intelligent-looking breed.

Size of parents is no guarantee of size of offspring. A 14-pound dog can produce a 25-pound son or daughter. Larger parents can produce smaller offspring. In selecting a puppy for a specific adult size range, the buyer should be able to rely on an experienced breeder, who has watched enough puppies grow up, to predict size. There are some weight/growth charts used by veterinarians that can predict, with a reasonable amount of accuracy, the adult size of a puppy based on its weight at a given age.

Bostons are defined by squareness: When viewed from the side, the length of the legs should equal the length of the body. This not only looks attractive, but helps ensure that the dog's movement will be sound. A too-short body or too-long legs will force the dog to adjust its gait—or stride—to avoid collisions between front and back legs. Over time, this abnormal movement can lead to abnormal joint stress, spinal problems and painful arthritis in old age.

Proportion is somewhat difficult to explain. Although related to the Bulldog and French Bulldog, the Boston's proportions are much more refined but not so refined as to resemble a terrier. The Boston is a "sturdy" dog, neither "spindly" nor "coarse."

Your Boston Terrier does not have to measure up to the AKC standard to be a wonderful companion.

HEAD

The skull is square, flat on top, free from wrinkles, cheeks flat, brow abrupt and the stop well defined.

If you've talked to breeders and fanciers about the Boston Terrier, you've likely heard them refer to it as a "head breed." The head is the most distinctive physical feature of the breed. It is what makes the dog a Boston Terrier. The muzzle is short, giving the head square proportions.

From the standpoint of health, this head shape does present some challenges, which are discussed in detail in Chapter 7, "Keeping Your Boston Terrier Healthy." A well-bred, healthy Boston can possess the correct, square head without experiencing serious or chronic health problems.

EXPRESSION

The ideal Boston Terrier expression is alert and kind, indicating a high degree of intelligence. This is a most important characteristic of the breed.

*The eyes are wide apart, large and round and dark in color.
The eyes are set square in the skull and the outside corners are
on a line with the cheeks as viewed from the front. Disqualify:
Eyes blue in color or any trace of blue.*

Expression has a lot to do with how the eyes look.
Many people think of Bostons as having protruding
eyes, or eyes that turn to the sides (called "walleyes" or
"east-west eyes"). In fact, a proper Boston has eyes that
are set well in the head, are not protruding and are
looking straight ahead. The eyes should show no white
around the irises. This gives the face a soft, friendly
and intelligent or knowing look.
Dogs with protruding eyes make
good companions, but they may be
prone to more problems with their
eyes, such as corneal injuries or
infections. With proper care and
precautions, most Bostons live their
entire lives without eye problems.

EYE COLOR

Eye color is also important in the
standard. The "proper" eye color is
dark brown, and most Bostons have
dark brown eyes. Occasionally you
do see Bostons with blue eyes. They
may have blue in one or both eyes,
or just a part of an eye. The blue
color is unusual in the breed, and
although some people find it cute,
it is not a "correct" color. Bostons
with any blue at all in their eyes are
disqualified from showing and
should not be bred. Once again, this is not a health or
soundness issue; rather it addresses the characteristics
that define a Boston Terrier.

> ### WHAT IS A BREED STANDARD?
>
> A *breed standard* is a detailed description of an individual breed. It describes the ideal specimen of that breed, including ideal structure, gait, type—all aspects of the dog. Because the standard describes an ideal specimen, it isn't based on any particular dog. It is a concept against which judges compare actual dogs and against which breeders strive to produce dogs. At a dog show, the dog that wins is the one that comes closest, in the judge's opinion, to the standard for its breed. Breed standards are written by the *breed parent clubs*, which are the national organizations formed to oversee the well-being of the breed. The standards are voted on and approved by the members of the parent clubs.

EARS

*The ears are small, carried erect, either natural or cropped to
conform to the shape of the head and situated as near to the
corners of the skull as possible.*

Now we come to one of the more controversial issues in the standard for the Boston Terrier: the ears. Bostons have naturally erect ears, unlike other breeds in which a naturally flopped ear is traditionally cropped to create an erect one. Although puppies' ears tend to flop forward or backward, once they reach six to eight months old and the worst of their teething is over, the cartilage in the ear hardens and the ears stand up straight. Correct ears stand straight up, sitting at the back corners of the skull. If the ears are set too low on the head, they tend to point to the sides, at an angle.

The controversy rages—as it always has—over ear cropping. This is one of only two surgical alterations allowed in the breed standard. (Dewclaws may also be removed, but tails are naturally short.) Many fanciers of the breed feel that a cropped ear is an essential part of the overall look or type that makes a Boston Terrier unique. It is customary to crop the ears only if the dog is being shown in conformation, and then it is not done until the puppy is at least ten months old, or nearly full-grown.

Traditionally, only Bostons who compete in shows have cropped ears, but cropping is a decision left up to the individual owner.

A growing number of Bostons are being shown with natural, uncropped ears, and they are winning in the ring. Increasingly, breeders in the United States are favoring dogs with correct, well-proportioned natural ears over dogs whose ears may have been cropped to hide flaws. Ears that are disproportionately large for the head are a flaw of appearance only, and they do not affect the health of the dog.

Ear cropping is not recommended for companion Boston Terriers.

MUZZLE

The muzzle is short, square, wide and deep and in proportion to the skull. It is free from wrinkles, shorter in length than in depth, not exceeding in length approximately one-third of the length of the skull. The muzzle from stop to end of the nose is parallel to the top of the skull. The nose is black and wide, with a well defined line between the nostrils. Disqualify: Dudley nose.

The jaw is broad and square with short, regular teeth. The bite is even or sufficiently undershot to square the muzzle. The chops are of good depth, but not pendulous, completely covering the teeth when the mouth is closed. Serious Fault: Wry mouth. Head Faults: Eyes showing too much white or haw. Pinched or wide nostrils. Size of ears out of proportions to the size of the head. Serious Head Faults: Any showing of the tongue or teeth when the mouth is closed.

As mentioned before, the head of the Boston Terrier is probably its most defining physical feature. It is a *brachycephalic head,* which means that the muzzle is exaggeratedly shortened, like that of the Bulldog, French Bulldog, Pug, or Pekingese, for example. But if you look closely at pictures of all those breeds, you will see certain differences in the heads. Basically, the head of the Boston Terrier is square. Viewed from the front or the side, it should look as if it was carved from a cube. The muzzle should be short, but not like that of a Bulldog, with its heavy jowls and pronounced underbite.

Boston Terriers are known for their short, square muzzles.

Dudley Nose

A *Dudley nose,* which is a disqualification, is a nose that shows any pink pigment at all. Sometimes puppies will start out with a pink nose or partially pink nose, which darkens to black as the puppy grows. This pigmentation does not affect the health of the dog in any way, and Bostons with Dudley noses make excellent companions.

Wry Mouth

A *wry mouth* is a misaligned bite, which may cause the tongue to hang out of the mouth or cause teeth to show when the mouth is closed. (This condition is not the same as when the dog's lip catches on a canine tooth, exposing that tooth temporarily.) In most cases, a wry mouth does not mean that the dog will be unhealthy. However, an extremely misaligned bite could lead to problems in eating, or to unusual tooth wear or decay.

NECK, TOPLINE, AND BODY

The next part of the standard describes the body, limbs and gait, or movement, of the Boston Terrier. The criteria address the *structure* of the body, how the parts fit and work together. Structural problems in a young dog can lead to injury or chronic pain later in life.

The length of the neck must display an image of balance to the total dog. It is slightly arched, carrying the head gracefully, and setting neatly into the shoulders. The back is just short enough to square the body. The top line is level and the rump curves slightly to the set-on of the tail. The chest is deep with good width, ribs well sprung and carried well back to the loins. The body should appear short. The tail is set on low, short, fine, and tapering, straight or screw and must not be carried above horizontal. (Note: The preferred tail does not exceed in length more than one-quarter the distance from set-on to hock.) Disqualify: Docked tail. Body Faults: Gaily carried tail. Serious Body Faults: Roach back, sway back, slab-sided.

A *roach back* or *sway back* may be a symptom of spinal injury. A roach back may also indicate a problem with the hips or patellas, causing the dog to carry most of its weight on its front legs to avoid discomfort. Dogs with roach backs can live long and happy lives, but they may require treatment, such as chiropractic adjustments or acupuncture, if they develop lameness or pain in their necks, backs or legs.

The shoulders are sloping and well laid back, which allows for the Boston Terrier's stylish movement. The elbows stand neither in nor out. The forelegs are set moderately wide apart and on a line with the upper tip of the shoulder blades. The forelegs are straight in bone with short, strong pasterns. The dew claws may be removed. The feet are small, round and compact, turned neither in nor out, with well arched toes and short nails. Faults: Legs lacking in substance; splay feet.

The thighs are strong and well muscled, bent at the stifles and set true. The hocks are short to the feet, turning neither in nor out, with a well defined hock joint. The feet are small and compact with short nails. Fault: Straight in stifle.

If a dog's structure is not correct, he may experience pain or injury at some point in his life.

The *stifles,* or knee joints, are bent. Straight stifles constitute a fault. Straight stifles usually accompany a condition called "luxating patellas," in which the kneecap slips out of place. This can be a very painful, debilitating condition that requires surgery and can lead to chronic arthritis. See Chapter 7 for more information.

Problems that are seen when the dog walks can indicate either inherited poor structure or an injury. If the parts don't move smoothly, arthritis can develop in the dog's joints later in life.

COAT, COLOR AND MARKINGS

The coat is short, smooth, bright, and fine in texture.

Brindle, seal, or black with white markings. Brindle is preferred ONLY if all other qualities are equal. (Note: SEAL DEFINED. Seal appears black except it has a red cast when viewed in the sun or bright light.) Disqualify: Solid black, solid brindle, or solid seal without required markings. Gray or liver colors.

13

Required Markings: White muzzle band, white blaze between the eyes, white fore chest.

Desired Markings: White muzzle band, even white blaze between the eyes and over the head, white collar, white fore chest, white on part or whole of forelegs and hind legs below the hocks . . . A dog with preponderance of white on the head or body must possess sufficient merit otherwise to counteract its deficiencies.

Color and markings set the Boston Terrier apart from similar breeds. You will notice that the standard describes "required markings" and "desired markings." A Boston is "required" to have a white blaze, muzzle band and chest. "Perfect" markings in a Boston means an even white blaze not touching the eyes, an even muzzle band, white chest extending all the way around the neck in a full white collar, and white socks halfway up the forelegs and up to the hocks on the back legs. The vast majority of Bostons do not possess "perfect" markings but still make wonderful companions.

Bostons have distinctive coat colors and markings. "Perfect" markings include a white blaze that touches neither eye.

Interestingly, quite a few early Bostons were all white or mostly white with some brindle markings. You will notice that "preponderance of white on the head or body" is not a disqualification or even a fault, although today you seldom see such a dog in the show ring. All white or mostly white Bostons make excellent companions, although they do lack the characteristic markings that make them look like they're wearing tuxedos.

TEMPERAMENT

The Boston Terrier is a friendly and lively dog. The breed has an excellent disposition and a high degree of intelligence, which makes the Boston Terrier an incomparable companion.

Boston Terriers are true companion dogs, bred specifically to be housepets. They should be easygoing and energetic, as ready to snooze with you on the couch as they are to chase a ball or go for a walk. They should be very sociable creatures, happy to see anyone—people, dogs or other animals. They are very smart and easy to train when the correct approach is used. (See Chapter 8 for more information on training.) Bostons may bark in play or when a visitor knocks on the door, but they are generally fairly quiet.

Summary

The clean-cut, short backed body of the Boston Terrier, coupled with the unique characteristics of his square head and jaw, and his striking markings have resulted in a most dapper and charming American original: The Boston Terrier.

Resources

American Kennel Club
5580 Centerview Dr.
Raleigh, NC 27606-3390
www.akc.org

Boston Terrier Club of America, Inc.
8537 East San Bruno Dr.
Scottsdale, AZ 85258

chapter 2

The **Boston Terrier's Ancestry**

Beginnings of the Breed

The ancestor of today's Boston Terrier was a dog named Judge. Imported from Liverpool in 1865 by his future owner, Mr. Hooper, Judge resembled the bulldog more than the terrier side of his breeding. He was tall and weighed about 30 pounds. We know from old records that Judge was a dark brindle with a white blaze and throat and a screw tail, although the records do not show who his parents were. Judge was bred to Mr. Burnett's stocky white female, Gyp, also probably imported from Liverpool. This breeding likely produced several puppies, but the puppy described from records as being the next in line in the Boston Terrier's development was one called Well's Eph. This puppy was a dark brindle dog with even markings, not as tall as his sire and weighing about 28 pounds. Eph was bred to Tobin's Kate, a golden-brindle female of about 20 pounds. We don't have any pedigree records on these dogs, but they were presumably either imported from Liverpool or descended from dogs imported from Liverpool.

The First Boston Terrier

Tom, a son of Eph and Kate owned by John P. Barnard, is considered by historians to be the first Boston Terrier and the true foundation of the breed. Tom weighed about 22 pounds and had a red brindle coat with a white blaze, collar, chest and feet. He had the typical screw tail we see today. Tom still probably resembled the Pit Bull or Staffordshire Terrier type, but he was closer to what we think of as a Boston. Records show that Tom was bred to a female called Kelley's Nell. Apparently, John Barnard took the pick of the litter as Tom's stud fee. That puppy, called Mike, is recorded as the first of these dogs to truly resemble the modern Boston Terrier. He was a light brindle with white markings, had the full round eyes favored today and weighed about 25 pounds.

The first Boston Terrier to resemble the Bostons we know today was born in the nineteenth century.

Early Coat Color and Markings

Most of the early dogs in this breed were primarily brindle with white markings. However, a few were mostly white, like Gyp. Gyp's great-grandson, Sullivan's Punch (Mike's son), and his daughter, Ch. Lady Dainty, were examples of white Boston Terriers that were considered excellent examples of the breed despite their color. To this day, breeders do occasionally produce puppies that are primarily white with some brindle markings. Although this color pattern is not considered desirable, these dogs are as nice as their brindle-and-white or black-and-white littermates (who are not primarily white). The standard for the breed does not define "preponderance of white on the body" as a disqualification, or even a fault. It is merely a "deficiency"; and if a white Boston possesses "sufficient merit otherwise," it could compete in conformation. However, most modern-day breeders do not show or breed the white dogs.

Boston's First Dog Show

Although some of their ancestors were mostly white, most Boston Terriers today have combination black-and-white coats.

In 1878, the first dog show was held in Boston, and several of these early dogs, then called "Bull Terriers," competed. By 1888, the Boston dog show provided a class for "round-headed bull terriers, any color," the designation for this breed at that time. John P. Barnard (owner of the famous Tom and Mike) judged that class

at the show. The name caught on, and for a while the breed was popularly called "round head" or "Boston Round Head." At about the same time, the name "Boston Bull" also became popular, though it might have referred to either the round-headed dogs or the brindle Bull Terrier, also developed in Boston. This nickname, although never part of the official name of the breed, remains in common use today, with many people incorrectly calling the breed "Boston Bull Terrier."

Forming the Breed Club

In 1890, a group of breeders of the early Boston Terriers formed a club and called themselves the American Bull Terrier Club. This club sought formal recognition from the AKC in 1891, but the AKC denied their application on the basis that the breed was not sufficiently well established at that time. Other groups of breeders who were also working to develop new "bull and terrier" breeds objected to the name, arguing that it was too general and should apply to their dogs, as well.

In 1893, the club changed its name and that of the breed to "Boston Terrier," and the Boston Terrier Club of America was admitted into membership in the AKC that same year. As these early breeders worked to establish the type—those qualities that make the Boston Terrier unique—the average size of the dogs decreased.

A Popular Dog

In the early part of the twentieth century, Boston Terriers became one of the most popular breeds in the United States, edging out the competition—Cocker Spaniels, Saint Bernards and Fox Terriers. From 1920 through 1963, a span of forty-three years, the Boston Terrier remained ranked among the top ten most popular breeds in the AKC, the only breed to ever hold that distinction.

In the city of Boston's first dog show, Boston Terriers competed under the name "Bull Terriers."

TOY BOSTONS?

During this time, changes in weight classes developed; and for a few decades, very small Bostons, weighing less than 10 pounds, were known as "Toy Boston Terriers." Although some Bostons are this small today, this size is considered too small for safe breeding and good health. Most Bostons bred and shown will range from 12 to 25 pounds.

Names of Note

Many of the famous names among Boston Terrier breeders of the late-nineteenth and early-twentieth centuries have faded into obscurity. A few, however, are still recognized today, including the Hagerty Boston Terrier Kennels, owned by A. Droll and Benny Rosenbloom. These kennels produced some excellent dogs, but they are probably best remembered for the characteristic marking shared by many of their dogs: a dark brindle or black spot centered in the white blaze on the top of the head. To this day, Boston Terrier fanciers refer to this spot as the "Hagerty Penny" or "Hagerty Spot."

The Boston Terrier Club of America was admitted into membership in the AKC in 1893. During this time, breeders worked hard to produce puppies who exemplified unique characteristics of the breed.

FAMOUS BOSTON TERRIER OWNERS

Yasmine Bleeth (actress)

Warren G. Harding (United States President)

Mary Roberts Rinehart (author)

Dolly Parton (singer)

Joey Mullen (hockey player)

Patricia Cornwell (author)

Marilyn Manson (musician)

Joan Rivers (comedian)

Other well-known kennel names are Royal, Regardless, Iowanna, Command, Ravenroyd and Kingway, the last continuing to produce fine Bostons today. Perhaps the most well known of the early breeders is Vincent Perry, whose involvement with the breed started in 1919 and continued until his death in 1985. His kennel was Globe, and he produced many famous show dogs, including Ch. Globe Glowing All By Himself and Ch. Globe Glowing Perfection. He is probably best known, however, as an all-breed dog show judge of high regard and as the author of many articles in various dog magazines. Mr. Perry was the author of the very popular *The Complete Boston Terrier,* which was published in many editions. Fanciers today collect editions of this book, and he is still considered an authority on the breed.

The well-known lines of today, based on those of a few generations ago, will in turn lead to and give way to other famous lines in the future. Some of the prominent lines of the late twentieth century include El-Bo, home of the late Ch. El-Bo's Rudy Is a Dandy; Staley, producer of Ch. Staley's El-Bo Showman; Zodiac, producer of Ch. Zodiac's Special Beau; and Saberton, sire of Ch. Do-Go Sunny of Sabe. All of these dogs have left a significant mark on the modern breed, but there are many more canine contributors, perhaps less well known but no less important.

It's easy to see why Bostons became so popular in the early-twentieth century.

chapter 3

The **World** According to the **Boston Terrier**

The Boston Terrier has been bred for more than 100 years to be a household companion. This is his job, what he does best. He should be eager to accompany his humans on outings and be a good ambassador, happily greeting one and all. The ideal Boston Terrier has never met a stranger. He greets everyone as a friend. He expects every human to offer kind words, a gentle pat or perhaps a special treat. Every other dog is a potential ally and playmate.

A Shorthaired American Gentleman

A nicely bred, carefully raised Boston will be friendly, outgoing, lively and easygoing. The nickname "American Gentleman" comes as much from the personality and temperament found in the breed as from the black-and-white markings suggesting formalwear.

The small size and short hair of Bostons make them easy to maintain and keep clean. Their dark coats and short muzzles, however, make them vulnerable to high temperatures. Even on a balmy spring day, the temperature in the sun or in a car can quickly become uncomfortable and quite dangerous for a Boston. It's a good idea for every Boston owner to be able to recognize and treat the beginning symptoms of heatstroke (see Chapter 7 for more information).

Their short hair and small size also make Bostons more vulnerable to extremely cold temperatures. Their sensitivity varies, with some Bostons loving cold weather and snow, and others trembling and making a beeline for the warm dog bed in the house. If I plan to be out in cold weather for more than a couple of minutes with one of my Bostons, I put a coat or sweater on the dog to help hold in his natural body heat. With such wonderful accessories available, there is no need to make winter outings unpleasant for your little friend.

Inquisitive and Intelligent

Bostons are naturally curious. They love to explore new places and follow their noses through fields and woods. Although they don't have the reputation for scenting ability that bloodhounds and beagles do, they can learn to use their noses, and some have even earned AKC tracking titles!

Because a Boston Terrier will follow his nose and follow anything that catches his interest, it is up to you to keep your pet safe. If you have a backyard, make sure it is securely fenced, and check the fence periodically to be sure that no new escape holes have developed. Keep him safely leashed when not in a fenced area. Before disconnecting the leash inside a new fenced area, walk the fence line to look for any openings that your dog might be tempted to squeeze through. And, most importantly, teach him to come when you call, every time, no matter what (see Chapter 8).

Bostons are extremely intelligent dogs who learn quickly. Those owners who use "traditional" training

Your Boston Terrier is very intelligent. He will respond well to positive reinforcement and rewards during training.

methods focusing on corrections, punishment and the use of a choke chain or prong collar commonly call the breed "stubborn" and "difficult to train." This is because the Boston Terrier typically does not respond to physical force in the same way that some other breeds (considered "obedience breeds") do. The collar corrections that are used to get the attention of larger dogs like Golden Retrievers may be viewed very differently by a Boston. He is likely to resist pressure with equal force, or he may interpret the choking sensation of a slip or chain collar as an attack against which he must defend himself. Furthermore, the spine of the Boston is prone to injury and could be damaged by the use of a choke chain and collar corrections. If you use the techniques outlined in Chapter 8 or in some of the books listed at the end of this chapter, you will find the Boston a willing and very responsive student.

Molding Your Boston

Each dog is an individual, and his personality will vary from others of the same breed or even from the same family. His personality is the product of many factors, including genetics (what his parents and grandparents were like), the environment in which he spent his first few weeks of life, and the environment of your house, where he now lives.

Your goal is to mold your Boston into a model citizen. Chapter 8 offers many great suggestions for doing that, and the suggestions can be carried out while you're ensuring that all of your pup's interactions with people are pleasant. Start by setting yourself up as the pack leader—the source of all food and other good things for your Boston. Establish the policy early that "Nothing in life is free." Your Boston will earn every meal he eats, every toss of the ball, every tug on the rope toy, and every scratch of his ears with good behavior and compliance with your commands. He will earn every walk by sitting politely while you attach his leash to his collar and while you open the door. He will sit quietly or lie down while you place his food bowl in his crate or on the floor. It doesn't matter what you ask him to do, whether it's a basic obedience command or a trick you have taught him. The point is that he earns what is valuable to him by compliance and good behavior.

Your Boston will be a better companion and more reliable and relaxed around people if his experiences are consistently happy. The pup that is alternately cuddled and punished can develop a sense that humans are unreliable, unpredictable and must be watched carefully and defended against. This world view can lead to unpleasant aggressive behavior and even biting. As Dr. Dunbar stresses in Chapter 8, by ignoring the behaviors you don't like and by rewarding the behaviors you do like, you will develop a well-mannered, reliable companion. Read that chapter carefully and follow Dr. Dunbar's suggestions for training. You will be very pleased with the results.

Genetics combined with his environment when he was a baby affect your puppy's personality today.

Gracious Greetings

Good manners include greeting people without jumping all over them. Even though Bostons are small and cute and won't knock over most people, they can be a danger to small children and elderly adults. In any case, they are capable of leaving muddy paw prints on clothing, tearing stockings and scratching or bruising human legs in the process of jumping up.

Jumping up in greeting is a very doggy behavior rooted in puppyhood. Puppies greet their mother and other adult dogs with a lick on the chin—a "kiss" in human terms. This kiss is a submissive behavior, the puppy acknowledging the older dog's authority. Puppies instinctively want to greet their human family members in the same way, and we reinforce this by picking them up and holding them to our faces saying, "Give us a kiss . . . *good puppy.*"

As they grow larger, we are less inclined to pick them up and hold them as we did when they were tiny. But their desire to kiss us remains, and so they jump, trying to

If you teach your puppy now not to jump up to greet people, you will be glad you did later when he is grown up.

reach our faces, asking us to pick them up. Sometimes we lean down and pet them, sometimes we pick them up for a kiss and sometimes we try to ignore them . . . and the jumping continues.

How can we turn this nuisance into a more polite greeting from our point of view? Sitting is a good thing, and a sitting dog isn't as likely to jump up. So, it's best to teach the pup to sit, using Dr. Dunbar's lure/reward system or Karen Pryor's click/treat system. Then practice approaching him, asking him to sit and rewarding him for complying. Next go outside and come back in the house, ignoring the jumping, stepping back so the jumping pup misses your legs and lands back on the floor. Then ask for the sit and reward it. If you consistently ignore the jumping and you continue to practice, the dog will learn that sitting is infinitely more rewarding and will stop jumping up to greet everyone.

Ouch!

Puppy nipping and biting is another natural doggy behavior that is unacceptable in human society. It is quite natural for puppies to nibble and nip at things that move, because this behavior is the beginning stirrings of their innate prey drive. In their litter, they nipped at their littermates and at their mother; and they learned by trial and error when, where and how hard to bite.

During weaning, many breeders will introduce puppies to solid food by dipping their fingers in it and letting the pups lick it off. This can teach the pups to focus on human hands as something that is appropriate for nibbling and chewing. Whether or not your puppy came from a breeder, it's up to you as the owner to start your puppy off right and set him straight about when, where and how hard to bite humans (these are trick questions—the answers are never, nowhere and not at all).

There is much advice offered, good and bad, about how to teach a puppy not to nip and bite. The advice I offer here has been tested on thousands of puppies of all breeds, including Boston Terriers. Dogs raised according to this method are significantly less likely to bite, even if a human accidentally hurts them. I originally learned this method from Dr. Dunbar many years, and many puppies, ago.

The best time to teach a puppy not to bite people is before he turns 4 months old, while he still has those needle-sharp puppy teeth. Choose a time when he is relaxed and relatively calm. Sit with him, petting him with one hand and playing with your fingers in his mouth with the other hand. If he bites hard, take both hands away and say "Ouch!" emphatically. Wait a couple of seconds, and start again. The pup should first gently lick your fingers and nibble a little, and then he will probably bite down again. Repeat the process a few more times, always taking both hands away and saying "Ouch." You are petting and praising the pup only when he is licking or nibbling lightly on your fingers. It won't take long for your puppy to catch on and avoid hard bites. Once he is consistently mouthing your fingers softly, you will change the rules of the game and say "Ouch" for any tooth contact at all.

A FEW WORDS ABOUT AGGRESSION

The Boston Terrier is descended from tough, ferocious dogs. Bulldogs were developed to work with butchers to engage and control steers and cattle—animals that were many times their own size and that could cause fatal injury if the dog was not quick or tough enough. The terriers that contributed their genes to the Boston's family pool were pit fighting dogs, fearless fighters of their own kind but completely harmless to humans. How these ferocious breeds were used to create the friendly, happy companion we know today is difficult to explain or understand. But throughout the generations, the dogs were selected as much for their easygoing, nonaggressive nature as for their type and structure.

If your Boston Terrier displays aggressive behavior, it may be best to consult a professional dog trainer. Punishing him yourself could lead to more serious problems.

Bostons can be aggressive toward other dogs, particularly when they are behind a fence or on a leash. This may be something the dog has learned, or it may be a genetic tendency. Regardless of its origins, this behavior is not typical of Bostons and is not to be considered acceptable. In many cases, this behavior can be changed by teaching the dog to focus on his owner and by rewarding the dog with praise and treats for ignoring the other dog or dogs. Under no circumstances should a dog be punished or corrected for this aggressive behavior by yanking on the leash, yelling at the dog or hitting the dog. The aggressive behavior is usually caused by fear, and punishment can increase the fear and thereby increase the aggression that the punishment was intended to stop.

If your Boston does display aggressive behavior toward you, other humans or other dogs, you should seek the services of a competent dog trainer or behavior specialist who will work with you to change the dog's behavior without resorting to punishment or correction of any sort. Before the training begins, the trainer or specialist will probably recommend a thorough vet exam to rule out physical causes for the aggressive behavior. Sometimes pain or illness can cause a dog that has always been peaceful to suddenly behave aggressively. Certain chemical imbalances in the body, such as low thyroid hormone levels or abnormalities of the liver, can trigger aggressive behavior in dogs. I have seen a few cases of Bostons who would suddenly and unaccountably "turn on" their owners and bite them severely, and every case of that type was attributed to a brain disorder causing seizures or seizure-type problems.

Aggressive behavior is not normal for Bostons. A Boston that does develop aggression should be checked thoroughly by a vet and put on a program of positive, reward-based behavior modification under the supervision of an experienced dog trainer, behavior specialist or Certified Veterinary Behaviorist.

> **TO FIND A GOOD DOG TRAINER**
>
> Ask your dog-owning friends for recommendations on dog trainers. Call trainers to ask whether you may observe their classes (if they say no, look elsewhere). Look for a trainer who is very positive, one who emphasizes praise and rewards for the dog's good behavior and avoids punishment or corrections for bad behavior.
>
> Many good trainers are members of the Association of Pet Dog Trainers. To contact this association and inquire about members in your area, call 1-800-PET-DOGS or visit their website at www.apdt.com.

Resources

Arden, Andrea. *Dog Friendly Dog Training*. New York: Howell Book House, 2000.

Donaldson, Jean. *The Culture Clash*. Oakland, Calif: James and Kenneth, 1996.

Dunbar, Ian. *Dog Behavior: An Owner's Guide to a Happy Healthy Pet*. New York: Howell Book House, 1999.

McConnell, Patricia. *The Cautious Canine: How to Help Dogs Conquer Their Fears*. Oakland, Calif: James and Kenneth, 1998.

Pryor, Karen. *Don't Shoot the Dog: The New Art of Teaching and Training*. Rev. ed. New York: Bantam, 1999.

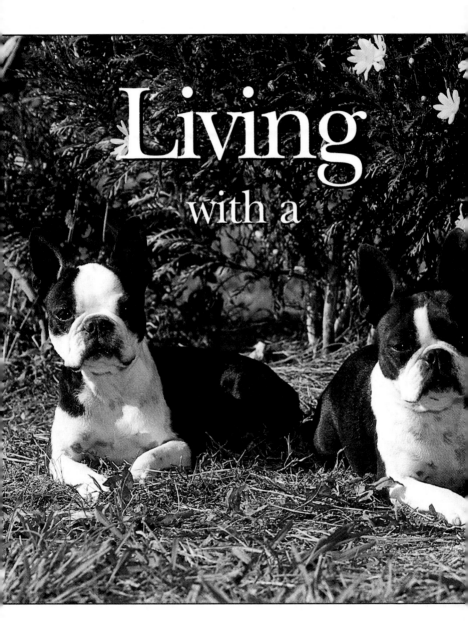

Living
with a

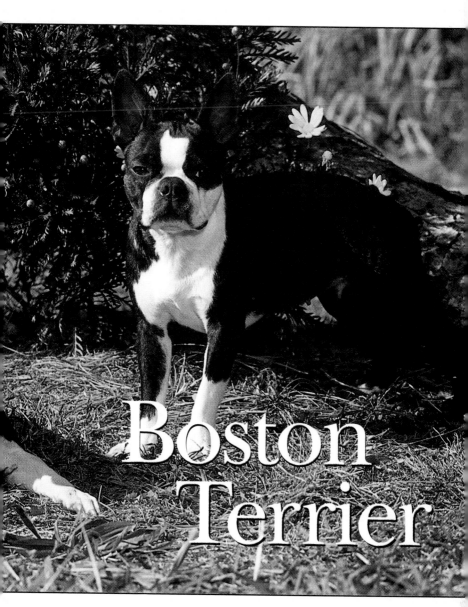

part two

Boston Terrier

chapter 4

Bringing Your Boston Terrier Home

Puppy or Adult?

Your choice of a young puppy or an older dog will depend on several factors. One is your lifestyle. Puppies require a good deal of time and patience, needing to go outside every one or two hours for elimination while they are awake and active. They also need to be fed more frequently than adult dogs. A puppy is a good choice if you are able to be at home to feed your puppy three times a day for the first few months or if someone else can come to your home during the day to care for your puppy while you are at work. Keep in mind the time and effort required for raising a puppy when making your decision.

Adult dogs have a lot of advantages: You know for a fact how big they'll be and whether they have any inherited health problems (see

Chapter 7 for more information). You'll have a pretty good idea of the dog's temperament and personality. The dog may have had some training and socialization before you got her, and she will most likely be housetrained.

Many people believe that a dog must be obtained as a young puppy in order for the dog to bond to its owner. Nothing could be further from the truth! The fact is that dogs who have had good experiences with people as young puppies will bond easily to a new owner at any age. I once took in a 12-year-old Boston whose owner had died. That dog bonded to me in a matter of hours and was my devoted companion until he passed away at age 14.

Male or Female?

As long as you are selecting a Boston to be a companion and not for show or breeding, gender is not that important and is a matter of personal preference. The differences between males and females are not very great. A male may have a tendency to lift his leg and "mark" inappropriately, but neutering and good housetraining help reduce this tendency.

Both male and female Boston puppies make wonderful housepets.

If you already have a dog and are planning to get another, your best option is to get one of the opposite sex. Two females together will have a greater tendency to argue, and even fight one another. Two males

33

together, in my experience, have a lesser tendency to fight, but it is still greater than that of a male and female together.

Where Should You Get Your Boston Terrier?

There are many sources for dogs and puppies, and some are better than others. If you have decided to get an older dog, you can start by contacting the Boston Terrier Club of America (BTCA) for information on a rescue program in your area. The BTCA can also help you find a local Boston Terrier club and can give you the names of breeders in your area, if you want to purchase a puppy.

Adopting an adult Boston is an excellent option for pet owners.

ADOPTING AN OLDER BOSTON

Expect the dog you adopt from a rescue group to be spayed or neutered already and to be current on vaccinations. She should have been kept in foster care long enough to determine whether she is housetrained, crate-trained and leash-trained, and to evaluate her temperament. If you have other pets in your home, the rescue group should offer you a Boston that has been tested and has been found to be friendly to other dogs, friendly or neutral to cats and neutral to birds or pocket pets, depending on what kinds of pets you already have.

PURCHASING A PUPPY FROM A BREEDER

If you choose to get your puppy from a breeder, try to get an idea of where she lives. Does her home appear to be a clean, safe, somewhat stimulating place? How is the mother? Does she look healthy? Is she friendly and outgoing, welcoming you in to see her babies? If you meet the father, is he also friendly and welcoming? A mother Boston that is wary of strangers or overly protective of her babies may be teaching the babies to be wary. Lessons learned at this young age from her mother or her breeder will stay with your dog for a very long time.

Bostons are house dogs and should be kept indoors in the family home. Puppies raised in kennels, barns, garages, basements or cages, away from family life and activities, may have difficulty adapting to their new homes. Puppies who grow up for the first eight or ten weeks as part of a family will make better family pets.

Whether your Boston puppy comes from a breeder or Santa Claus, she should be at least 7 weeks old when she comes to live with you.

How Old Should the Puppy Be?

Puppies go through some critical developmental stages and should be kept with their littermates until they are at least 7 weeks old. Many behavior problems in dogs seem to be the result of separating from their litters before this age. It is during the first seven weeks that a puppy learns from her mother about proper doggy behavior, social interactions and body language. This education is continued in the new home, where your puppy will learn from you how to interact properly with humans, the cat and other pets. Puppies separated from their mother and littermates before the age of 7 weeks may display more fear of new things and more fear of other dogs, behaviors that can develop into aggressiveness or other problems.

Preparing for the New Arrival

Before you bring your puppy home, you will need to do some shopping. Your little newcomer will have special requirements, much like a newborn baby. The right puppy food, bowls and dishes, bedding and toys are all items to be gathered.

SUPPLIES YOU WILL NEED

Find out ahead of time what your puppy is eating, so that you can have the same food available when you bring her home. You may receive a small quantity of food when you pick up your puppy, but it is best to be prepared.

Bowls

A crate can become your puppy's personal escape from the world instead of a dreaded punishment area.

You'll need bowls for food and water. Stainless steel is lightweight, easy to clean and resistant to puppies who want to chew. A 1-quart bowl is large enough for food, and a 2-quart bowl should hold enough water for one dog.

Crate

Your puppy should have a crate for sleeping in and for riding in the car. Most puppies are comfortable in a relatively small crate (21" by 17" by 16"), and most adult Bostons are comfortable in a medium crate (27" by 20" by 19"). Crates are available in a wide range of types and prices. I prefer the molded-plastic, airline-style crates because they will keep your floor clean and they afford a bit more privacy to the dog. They tend to be less expensive and lighter weight than the wire crates. Wire crates have the advantage of folding down for easy storage when not in use.

I recommend placing small pieces of a washable blanket or towels in the crate for bedding, realizing that puppies tend to chew on their bedding and may destroy it. Once a puppy has outgrown the desire to chew (at about a year and a half), you can invest money in fancier bedding, if you wish.

Leash and Collar

Your puppy will need a leash and collar for walking safely with you. A 6-foot long, lightweight cotton or nylon leash with a small clasp will work best, teamed with a flat buckle collar that allows room for growth. Quick-snap collars, which are easy to snap on and off, are convenient, but they must be kept out of the puppy's reach because the snap is tempting to chew and is easily destroyed by sharp puppy teeth. Don't forget to add a tag with your name, phone number and address so that if your puppy gets lost, whoever finds her can return her safely to you.

> **SUPPLIES FOR YOUR NEW PUPPY**
>
> 1-quart stainless-steel food bowl
>
> 2-quart stainless-steel water bowl
>
> 6-foot leash (nylon or cotton web)
>
> Flat buckle collar
>
> ID tag
>
> Food
>
> Crate
>
> Washable bedding
>
> Baby gates
>
> White vinegar
>
> Club soda
>
> Spray bottles
>
> Paper towels
>
> Appropriate chew toys

Your puppy will not need a choke chain, a nylon slip collar or a prong collar. These devices are used by some trainers but are unnecessary for the Boston. (See Chapters 3 and 8 for more information on training methods and equipment.) Several veterinary chiropractors have told me that using slip or choke collars on Bostons—or pulling on any leash and collar—can cause serious spinal injury and should always be avoided.

Toys

Toys that the puppy can play with, chase and chew will help occupy her time, energy and attention. You will find a wide variety of dog toys available in most pet supply stores or from mail-order catalogs or the Internet.

The best toy for dogs, in my opinion, is the Kong, a hard-rubber, hollow, beehive-shaped toy that bounces in different directions, giving the dog something interesting to chase. It is a very durable toy and can be stuffed with dog biscuits, peanut butter, cheese and other edible treats to occupy the puppy while she is spending quiet time in her crate.

Softer toys made of artificial fleece will satisfy certain chewing needs and give your puppy an outlet for "killing" and dissecting "prey"—a normal puppy pastime. These toys come in many shapes and sizes, and most have squeakers or noisemakers to attract the pup's attention. Many puppies will start by removing the squeaker. This seems to be a universal behavior and is not considered abnormal. Just be sure to take away any small pieces that could be swallowed or could choke your puppy.

To keep your Boston Terrier from nibbling at shoes and chair legs, she should have enough toys to satisfy her chewing urge.

Semihard toy bones and chew toys made of various materials and scented to attract a dog can be appealing for many puppies. However, be sure that you check with your veterinarian about these and read labels carefully, since some of these toys can be broken up and swallowed by the puppy and could cause digestive upset or blockage. Some toys are labeled with the word *ingestible,* which simply means that they could be swallowed; this doesn't mean that the puppy's digestive system will process them as if they were food (*digestible*).

You will also find many natural chew toys available for sale, such as cow hooves, rawhides, bones and pig ears, among other things. Many of these are very appealing to dogs, but some are safer than others. Your best sources of information on their safety are your veterinarian and your puppy's breeder. Toys that can break into pieces could choke a dog or block or puncture the digestive tract if swallowed. Some are processed with chemicals that may be hazardous to your dog. Others have an odor that dogs consider ambrosia, though their owners may find it offensive. Raw beef bones, especially marrow bones, long rib bones and neck bones, provide hours of recreational chewing for growing puppies and adult dogs.

Cleanup Supplies

For indoor cleanup of puppy "accidents," you will need a good odor-and-stain remover. You can make your own odor remover by mixing equal parts of white vinegar and plain water in a spray bottle, or you can purchase a commercial product that breaks down puppy odors. Club soda or seltzer will be very helpful for removing stains from carpets or upholstery.

For backyard cleanup, you will probably want a set of poop scoops with long handles; the long handles save your back from having to bend over too frequently. For walks away from home or for travel, I keep zip-lock plastic bags in my pocket or purse.

Baby Gates to Control Access

One or two baby gates, available through pet supply outlets or children's furniture retailers, can be very useful. You can use them to confine your puppy to a certain area, such as the family room or kitchen, and to prevent her from having access to the front door and escaping when it is opened. You can also use baby gates to keep your puppy away from the stairs until she is big enough to safely climb up and down without help. Baby gates are a management tool, rather than a training tool. They will not teach your puppy to stay in or out of a specific area. In fact, most of the time when the baby gates are removed, she will dart through the doorways where they have been.

PREVENT CHEWING DISASTERS

Having sufficient and varied chew toys for your puppy or adult dog will help protect your valued belongings from destruction. You can also use a commercial product, designed to be applied to furniture, plants or other objects, that tastes bad to most dogs and stops their desire to chew on the object. These taste deterrents must be reapplied frequently, sometimes daily, so check them regularly and reapply if your Boston starts to chew on the object.

Chew toys will not only keep your puppy from ruining your belongings, but they also act as decoys for dangerous chewables, such as electric wires and phone cords.

Electrical cords provide a deadly temptation to puppies, who are attracted by the scent and texture of the insulation. The cords should be gathered up and kept out of reach as much as possible, or regularly treated with the taste deterrent. Dangling cords, such as phone cords, computer cords, etc., offer the temptation to chew, as well as the danger of entanglement. A puppy tangled in a computer cord could pull your system over, wrecking it and risking injury to herself.

For excellent advice on training your puppy or dog not to chew on your belongings, please read what Dr. Dunbar has to say on the subject in Chapter 8.

PLANNING FOR YOUR BOSTON TERRIER

Now that you have all the supplies you will need, it's time to make some plans. When will she go to the vet for vaccinations and checkups? When and where will she sleep? When and where will she eat? When will she go outside?

Location, Location, Location

Think about your house and your lifestyle: Where do you spend most of your time when you're not asleep? That is where your Boston will spend most of her daylight hours, too. That is where her crate should be for daytime quiet periods or naps. That is where her toys should be, and her bed.

Dogs are by nature pack animals, very social creatures. To them the pack means safety, security, food, warmth and fun. Isolation is one of the worst things that can happen to a dog. This is why your puppy will follow you from room to room, and why she may cry if she is left alone or shut away from the family in a separate room.

It is fine to let your Boston puppy play in your yard, provided that a fence in good repair surrounds the area.

Because of this pack instinct and the need to be with the family, you will want to avoid plans that isolate your Boston in a room away from the rest of the household. Especially during the housetraining phase, many people think the ideal solution is to shut the dog in a bathroom or laundry room, where accidents will cause the least damage. But in doing so, you may be exchanging one form of damage for another, possibly developing a dog who is anxious about being left behind, or one who doesn't learn good manners in the rest of the house, or who doesn't bond completely with the rest of the family. With thoughtful planning, you can allow your new family member to be a part of the pack from

41

the beginning, learning good manners and being a great family companion.

Use your Boston's crate to help her learn to settle down and have "quiet time," as well as to keep her out of trouble when you cannot supervise her. Keeping her crate open and available near the center of family activity allows her to choose to go in and relax on her own, as well as to feel a part of the family even when confined. The baby gates, mentioned earlier, can be used to help keep your Boston with the family, preventing her from wandering off by herself to explore and make mistakes.

Schedules

Whether you are starting with a puppy or an older Boston, you will want to establish a routine and a schedule from the beginning in order to help your new family member adjust to life with you and to help her master housetraining. In setting up the schedule, consider your own schedule: When do you go to work? When do the kids go to school? What time do you get home? What time do you go to bed and get up? When do you eat your meals?

An adult Boston should eat twice a day, whereas a puppy younger than 6 months should eat three times a day.

Mealtimes

You will want to schedule two meals a day for your Boston. If she is younger than 6 months old, she should be eating three times a day. The meals should be relatively evenly spaced, but that may conflict with the household schedule. If your puppy is waking you up too early in the morning, you can try to adjust her feeding schedule, putting out her evening meal a little later so she doesn't get hungry so early in the morning.

Elimination

Whether you are bringing home a puppy or an adult Boston, you will want to set up a schedule for allowing opportunities to eliminate outside. Obviously, you should take her outside as soon as she wakes up in the morning, and as soon as she wakes up from a long nap. Most dogs feel the need to eliminate shortly after they eat, so plan to take her out right after every meal. Very young puppies usually have to urinate about once an hour when they are awake and active. Of course, these same very young puppies also spend most of the day sleeping.

If you are housetraining a very young puppy, it is a good idea to confine the pup to a relatively small space by using an exercise pen. You can place the puppy's crate, with the door open, at one end of the pen, and a toilet area at the other end. For the toilet area, some people use newspapers, but I prefer a low-sided plastic box (larger than a cat's litter box) filled with bark mulch. The puppy will probably chew on the mulch, but it won't hurt her; and the mulch smells and feels like "outside," giving your pup a head start on housetraining. For more information on housetraining, see Chapter 8, as well as the "Resources" section at the end of this chapter.

KEEP YOUR DOG SAFE FROM POISONS

In planning to bring your dog home, be sure that all poisonous substances are out of reach, whether in the house, the back-yard or the garage.

Be especially careful of substances that are attractive to dogs but pose a deadly threat, such as automobile antifreeze, chocolate and poison baits for rodents or insects. Read all labels on cleaning products and pesticides, as well as on lawn and garden products, and take appropriate precautions.

In addition to keeping these things out of reach, keep your dog off your lawn after chemicals are applied, either by you or by a lawn service. Follow all directions carefully when using chemicals around the house and yard, and dispose of all waste properly.

Bringing Your Boston Home

When you bring your new companion home, the first stop should be at her designated toilet area. Let her sniff around, and be prepared to praise and reward her with a tiny treat if she urinates or defecates in the appropriate place. Once that is out of the way, take her into the house and show her where her water dish is. Allow her to explore a little, but watch her carefully in order to prevent accidents or chewing.

At her first mealtime in her new home, feed her a small amount, rather than her usual portion. The excitement of the car ride and the new home may have dampened her appetite or upset her stomach a little. Immediately after feeding her, take her outside to her toilet area to eliminate. Give her every opportunity to earn praise and rewards!

When she starts to tire, introduce her to her sleeping area, but don't expect her to love it immediately. If you've brought a towel or blanket from her previous home, put that in her bed to give her some familiar smells. Do what you can to make her comfortable, and let her sleep in her bed. If she's a young puppy, she'll need lots of sleep, so avoid waking her up if she is snoozing.

Your puppy will want to be near you, so place her bed in a room where you spend a good amount of time.

Introducing Your New Boston to Other Pets

Other Dogs

If you already have a dog (or dogs) in your home and you are bringing home a new Boston puppy or adult, it's best to start introductions outdoors whenever possible. First, take the new dog to her designated toilet area as already described. Then bring the older dog outside to meet the newcomer. Praise both dogs for happy greetings and civilized behavior.

Good Greetings

If your young puppy rolls on her back and urinates a little in response to the sniffing of the older dog, be glad! This is normal puppy behavior, and it tells the older dog, "I'm just a baby, and I don't want any trouble." It is a good idea to have some understanding of doggy body language before introductions are made, so that you know what is appropriate and what is not. For more information, see Turid Rugaas's book, listed at the end of this chapter.

Once introductions and greetings have been made, you can allow a short playtime in your fenced backyard. If you do not have a secure fence, *do not* take leashes off the dogs outdoors! Take the dogs in the house, and let them go through the greeting ritual again inside.

With proper introductions, your new Boston should get along just fine with other pets.

First Mealtime with the New Puppy

At mealtime, feed both dogs in their crates. This strategy will ensure that there are no arguments over the food and that the puppy gets her whole meal. If you are introducing a younger puppy to an older dog, you can allow the older dog to help you teach the younger one about appropriate elimination by taking both dogs outside to the toilet area after the meal.

Introducing a Cat

If you already have a cat, you will want to introduce your new Boston carefully. Start with the new dog on leash, in a relaxed environment where you can pay attention to everything that is going on. Ensure that your cat has a mode of escape from the dog, either a baby gate over which the cat can jump or a high place onto which the cat can climb and be out of reach of the dog.

The introduction will work best if the cat is still, not running around or running away. The less activity on the cat's part, the less likely the dog will want to chase it. Praise and pet or reward the dog for being still and quiet, and looking at you. If you praise and reward the dog every time she looks at you after looking at the cat, she will start to pay more attention to you than to the cat. Avoid reprimanding or punishing her for chasing or approaching the cat. You will accomplish what you want much faster if you praise and reward the dog for staying calm or for looking at you.

What About Birds and Pocket Pets?

Always keep small pets safely locked away in their habitats when an adult cannot supervise the interaction with the dog. Start by training your dog in basic commands, including "sit," "down" and "come here," following the advice in Chapter 8. When your dog is very reliable in these commands, introduce the bird or small pet under close supervision, with the dog on leash, lavishly praising and rewarding the dog for obeying your commands, rather than for expressing interest in the small animal. As with the cat introductions, avoid reprimanding or punishing her for approaching or chasing the little guy, and reward the appropriate behavior. Never ever leave any dog unattended around birds or tiny pets.

Resources

Morn, September. *Housetraining: An Owner's Guide to a Happy Healthy Pet.* New York: Howell Book House, 1999.

Rugaas, Turid. *On Talking Terms with Dogs: Calming Signals.* Kula, HI: Legacy By Mail, 1997.

Feeding
Your Boston
Terrier

A Balanced Diet

Your Boston Terrier depends on you to provide proper, balanced nutrition. A healthy diet contributes immeasurably to the good health of your dog. Much research has been done on the balance of nutrients, vitamins and minerals needed to maintain good health in dogs.

Nutritional deficiencies or overloads may cause serious health problems. Dietary imbalances in protein, calcium and phosphorus can affect a puppy's growth and development, leading to painful debilitation. Proper nutrition ensures that the dog's body gets all of the building blocks, in the right proportion, that the dog needs for growth and maintenance.

Feeding dogs is not a simple matter of opening a bag or can and filling a bowl. Every dog has different nutritional needs, and each thrives on a somewhat different combination of foods and nutrients.

47

Like people, some Bostons have a higher metabolism, or level of energy, and they burn more calories, meaning that they need to eat more to keep their weight at the ideal level. Others need a lower-calorie diet because they tend to put on weight. Some dogs enjoy excellent health on a diet that includes a variety of protein sources or grains, whereas others require a more limited diet because of food allergies or sensitivities.

The more you know about dog food and feeding options, the healthier your dog will be.

So Many Choices

The options available for feeding a dog today abound in numbers almost as great as the number of dogs. There are hundreds of brands of commercial dog food,

available in three basic types: dry, canned and semimoist. Within these types are different formulas for puppies, adult dogs, active dogs and older dogs. Some brands even vary their formulation according to the type of dog. You will also find formulas created to meet specific health needs,

Decide on a food that is both palatable and healthful for your dog.

such as allergies, heart problems, kidney problems, digestive problems and cancer. You also have the option of creating your own diet for your dog by using fresh foods available at the grocery store.

COMMERCIAL DOG FOOD

The majority of dog owners in the United States today feed their dogs commercial dog food, whether dry kibble, canned or semimoist formulas. Each has its advantages and drawbacks. What is best for your Boston?

Commercial dog food varies greatly in quality and nutritional value. In selecting a commercial diet for your dog, you should learn to read the labels and understand the major ingredients. The manufacturers of commercial pet foods follow voluntary guidelines that say what is or isn't permitted to be included in pet food. There is no government regulation.

This lack of federal regulation is why you will see such wide variation in the lists of ingredients from one label to another. You will also find, if you research the information available on dog food, that many of the ingredients used are considered either unfit for human consumption or are banned from use in human food production.

Ingredients are listed in a specific order, starting with the largest amount and ending with the smallest amount. By looking at the first three ingredients listed, you can see what the primary nutritional sources of that dog food are.

Is the first ingredient an animal protein of some sort? Or is it a grain product? Dogs are considered *omnivores*—they derive nutrition from several food groups, including animal protein, vegetables and fruits. A good balanced diet has a significantly higher amount of animal protein than it has of all the other food groups. Most dogs, on average, do best when fed a diet that is primarily animal protein, such as chicken, beef, lamb, turkey and sometimes venison, duck or fish.

Good proteins keep your dog feeling healthy and looking beautiful.

If your dog's food contains no sources of animal protein in the first three ingredients, you may want to start reading more labels and look for a different dog food—unless you have specifically chosen a vegetarian formula for your dog.

I recommend commercial foods that use human-grade ingredients, that list meat protein sources among the first three ingredients, that do not include by-products and that do not include chemical preservatives such as BHT, BHA and ethoxyquin or chemical food colorings. For more information on how to read labels on commercial dog food and to understand what is in dog food, please see "Resources" at the end of this chapter.

Dry Dog Food

Most dog owners who feed commercial diets use primarily dry kibble. This is the most economical form of dog food. The moisture has been removed, so you as a consumer aren't paying for water. If you do feed kibble, be sure that you provide plenty of fresh clean water for your dog to drink. It is not a bad idea to dress the kibble by moistening it with warm water, or by stirring in a little low-fat yogurt, cottage cheese or scraps from your own supper. Dr. Pitcairn's book, listed at the end of this chapter, includes excellent suggestions for increasing the nutritional value of kibble by adding fresh food.

One of the disadvantages of using dry kibble is that it has a limited shelf life. Unless antioxidant preservatives are added to the food or to the ingredients used in the food, it will tend to spoil, becoming rancid or moldy. The preservatives most commonly used in animal feed are the chemicals BHA, BHT and ethoxyquin. Although these chemicals are not used in human food in the same way, because they are recognized as carcinogens, they are nevertheless permitted in animal feed. As pet-owning consumers have become more vocal in their concern over the use of these chemicals, many manufacturers have replaced them with less-toxic antioxidants, such as Vitamin E, tocopherols and Vitamin C. While these replacements are considered safer, they do increase the manufacturing cost. Also, their shelf life is shorter. The end result is a higher-priced dog food.

Another disadvantage of dry kibble is that it is usually cooked at a high temperature for a longer time than canned food. The higher temperatures and longer cooking times are needed to destroy bacteria that might be in the ingredients used to make the food, but they also destroy much of the nutritional value of the food. Manufacturers usually compensate for this loss by adding vitamins and minerals back into the food.

Canned Dog Food

Canned food is another option in feeding a commercial diet. The first ingredient in this type of food is typically water. Canned food is thus more expensive because, in order to provide sufficient nutrition, you must feed it in larger volume than you would kibble. Since canned food is cooked at much higher temperatures than other forms, it tends to contain fewer chemicals and preservatives than either dry or semimoist foods. However, the high temperature can cause canned food to lose a great deal of its nutritional value.

Semimoist Dog Food

Semimoist foods are popular with some dog owners because of the convenience and the appealing appearance and texture. The semimoist texture is created by adding *propylene glycol*, which is a sugar that stays soft at room temperature. This chemical also serves as a preservative to increase the shelf life of the food. Semimoist dog food tends to contain more chemical dyes, because dyes are used to create the different colors of the pieces of food, or to simulate the appearance of fresh hamburger.

Because the first ingredient in canned food is usually water, it is more expensive and less efficient than the dry kibble these puppies are enjoying.

We know how excess sugar and food dyes affect humans. These ingredients can have a similar effect on dogs, increasing their excitability. In my dog behavior counseling practice, I have encountered many dogs with behavior problems that were partially or completely solved by changing from a semimoist dog food to a high-quality kibble or a fresh food diet. Eating lots of sugar can also cause weight gain and tooth decay in dogs, just as it does in humans.

SELECTING HEALTHY COMMERCIAL PRODUCTS

Look at the package label for indications of higher quality. Listings of lamb, chicken, beef or turkey indicate that meat of that specific species is included in the food. Terms like "meat," "meat by-products," or "meat meal" suggest that various species may be included, and these may not be the healthiest sources of protein for your Boston Terrier. A label that lists human-grade or USDA-approved ingredients is an indication of higher quality in a dog food.

Expect to pay more for healthier foods. You will get what you pay for, and you'll see improved health and vigor in your Boston if you spend a little more for higher-quality foods with fresher, whole ingredients and fewer chemicals.

TO SUPPLEMENT OR NOT TO SUPPLEMENT?

Food supplements include vitamins and minerals, as well as table scraps. If you're feeding your dog a diet that's correct for his developmental stage, and he's alert, healthy looking and neither over-nor underweight, you don't need to add supplements. In fact, unless you are a nutrition expert, using food supplements can actually hurt a growing puppy. For example, mixing too much calcium into your dog's food can lead to musculoskeletal disorders. Educating yourself about the quantity of vitamins and minerals your dog needs to be healthy will help you determine what needs to be supplemented. If you have any concerns about the nutritional quality of the food you're feeding, discuss them with your veterinarian.

Supplementing Commercial Diets

If supplementing is the right choice for you and your Boston, it is important to make sure you neither over- or undersupplement. A discussion with your vet may be the best bet when planning your Boston's supplements.

Over- or undersupplementation can lead to health problems. Reading labels will help you decide what, if any, supplementation might be beneficial.

Commercial powdered supplements are available to boost or increase the nutrition in commercial foods. You can also supplement commercial food with fresh ground meat, cottage cheese, yogurt, eggs or other fresh foods. Check the recipes in the books at the end of this chapter, especially Dr. Pitcairn's book, for help with supplementation.

HOME COOKING FOR YOUR BOSTON

In their quest to encourage optimal health in their beloved companions, an increasing number of dog owners and breeders are turning to diets of fresh food, either cooked or raw. The advantage of such diets is that more nutrients are available to the dog than in overcooked commercial diets made from inferior ingredients. The home-prepared diet can be adjusted and fine-tuned to meet your dog's specific needs. Most dogs enjoy better health when fed freshly prepared food, just as humans thrive better on fresh foods than on canned or frozen prepared food. Owners who are feeding the "bones and raw food," or "BARF," diet are also finding that their dogs' teeth and gums are much cleaner and healthier, reducing or eliminating the need for teeth cleaning under anesthesia.

The disadvantages are that a fresh diet does take more time and effort to prepare, and may be more expensive to feed on a daily basis. However, most owners who have selected this option agree that the improvements they see in their dogs' health and vigor far outweigh these inconveniences. They feel that the additional cost and effort in feeding a fresh diet are balanced by lowered bills for veterinary care.

Most fresh diets are based on fresh, ground or chopped meat as the primary ingredient. Some include cooked whole grains, such as brown rice, barley, oat-meal or millet. Most include some fresh vegetables, either raw or lightly cooked, and cut up or finely ground. A little experimentation will help you choose the best type of fresh diet for your particular dog. One of the keys to ensuring proper, balanced nutrition in a home-prepared diet is to include as much variety as possible. Use different types of meat (chicken, beef, lamb, turkey, etc.), a variety of grains (if you choose to

Many owners who make their dogs' food report positive health benefits.

feed grains) and a broad array of fresh vegetables and fruits. Experts seem to agree that a balanced diet includes about 60 percent meat (and bones, in some cases) and 40 percent vegetables, fruits and grains.

The "Resource" section at the end of this chapter includes several books that provide guidelines and recipes for making your dog's food in your own kitchen from ingredients you purchase at your local supermarket.

Different Foods for Different Ages

In looking at the variety of commercial dog foods, you will see that different formulas are offered for puppies, adult dogs, high-energy or hard-working dogs, overweight dogs and older dogs. Puppies are burning a lot of calories just in growing and tend to need more calories relative to their size than adult dogs do. Dogs that compete in sports events, such as obedience, agility or flyball, may also need more calories per day than normal adult dogs. Older dogs usually need fewer calories.

Growing puppies usually need more protein and fat in their diets than do adults, who have finished growing and no longer require the extra calories.

Some people also believe that older dogs need lower protein levels than younger dogs, although this is the subject of much controversy. Essentially, older Bostons that are in good health, with normal results on blood tests, can and should eat the same food as younger adult dogs.

Reduced protein diets may be appropriate for dogs with impaired kidney function, as diagnosed by a veterinarian, but such diets are not necessarily appropriate for older dogs that are basically healthy.

If you are feeding commercial food, select a brand that uses high-quality ingredients first; then select the variety that is appropriate for your puppy, adult or elderly Boston. Some of the premium brands offer only one variety, and they recommend feeding more food to puppies and less to elderly dogs than you would feed to normal adult dogs.

Many brands of "senior" or "lite" foods rely on fillers such as cellulose (sawdust) to reduce the calorie or protein content of the food. This type of food may not be the healthiest option for your overweight or older Boston. In reading labels, you will find that a few brands do not use these fillers; instead they change the balance of the high-quality ingredients to make them appropriate for dogs with special needs.

If you are feeding a fresh diet, you should consult the appropriate books for guidance on feeding puppies or older dogs. In general, growing puppies will need a larger quantity of fresh food than adults, with perhaps more protein and fat than adults. Older or overweight dogs will need a smaller quantity of food, with perhaps more vegetables than adult dogs. All of them will benefit from snacks and treats of fresh fruits and vegetables, rather than dog biscuits or meaty treats.

Foods to Avoid

The list of foods Boston Terriers can enjoy is quite long, and the list of "no-nos" is short, but important. The three foods that you must never feed your Boston Terrier are chocolate, onions and cooked bones. Chocolate contains theobromine and caffeine, which can cause vomiting, rapid breathing, seizures and sometimes death. Onions contain a substance that can break down red blood cells, leading to a very serious condition called *heinz body hemolytic anemia*. Symptoms can include pale gums, blood in the urine, lethargy, depression, weakness and rapid heartbeat. The symptoms usually appear a few days after the onions have been eaten, when the toxin has destroyed a significant number of the dog's red blood cells. Onions are toxic in any form: raw, cooked or dehydrated. Although raw bones are usually safe for most dogs, cooking makes the bones brittle, which means that they can splinter. The resulting sharp edges can puncture the lining of the digestive tract, leading to dangerous infection and illness.

Where and When Should I Feed My Boston?

Like people, dogs appreciate eating a meal without interruption, in a quiet spot, and at a regular time. And, just as for people, good manners make mealtime more enjoyable.

You may want to request that your dog sit while he is waiting for his food. Sitting may keep him from barking and driving you crazy while you are getting his meal ready.

WHERE?

Select a location for your dog that is out of the way but not isolated. Although it is only for a few minutes a day, your Boston should enjoy his meals without the interruption of people walking past or stepping over him while he eats. Feeding your Boston in the same place every time helps establish good mealtime habits for your dog. You can ask him to sit or lie down before you place the bowl on the floor. This technique helps teach your dog to sit by his place to await his meals, and it reduces his tendency to want to run around like a maniac or bark at you while you are preparing meals.

WHEN AND HOW OFTEN?

I recommend feeding dogs, and especially Bostons, twice a day. It is easier for dogs to obtain enough nutrition from their food when it is fed in two meals. These mealtimes should be scheduled, whenever possible, after the human family members have eaten their meals, because the leader in a canine pack always eats first.

No Free Lunch

Many dog owners feed one continuous meal—called *free feeding*—keeping a full bowl of food available at all times. I do not recommend this practice for several reasons. Although some dogs are able to regulate their own food intake, too many are prone to overeating. Weight is difficult to control in dogs that are free-fed. When food is available all the time, the food tends to lose its importance and the dog has a harder time identifying the source of the food—his human companions. Finally, many cases of food-bowl guarding, which can lead to dangerous aggression toward other animals or people, begin with a perpetually available bowl of food.

Feed your Boston twice a day, at more or less regularly scheduled times (it's okay to sleep in on your day off and delay the weekday crack-of-dawn feeding schedule). Place the bowl in a specific spot, first asking the dog to sit or lie down before you put down the bowl. Allow your Boston no more than 20 minutes to eat his meal (most learn to eat in less than 5 minutes!) before you pick up the bowl.

Bowls

There are many varieties of food bowls to choose from, including ceramic, crockery, plastic and stainless steel. I prefer stainless steel because it is lightweight and easy to clean and disinfect. Plastic bowls are easy and tempting for the dog to chew. Some dogs have had allergic reactions to plastic bowls, with reactions including discoloration of the nose pad or acne around the muzzle. Crockery bowls tend to be heavy and less convenient to pick up and wash. Ceramic bowls are attractive but very breakable.

Stainless steel is the best bet for food and water bowls because such bowls are both durable and easy to clean.

57

A further disadvantage of ceramic or crockery bowls is the possibility of lead in the glaze, which can cause lead poisoning in your Boston.

My own dogs eat from quart-sized stainless steel bowls, and I keep a 3-quart stainless steel bowl filled with fresh, filtered water available at all times.

A Word About Water

Dogs should have fresh drinking water available at all times. This is especially true for Bostons, who are prone to overheat in warm weather and thus need plenty of water to protect against that. For my own large family of Bostons, I find that a 3-quart bowl holds just enough to require filling at least twice a day (three times a day in warmer weather). For most households with one or two Bostons, a 2-quart bowl is probably large enough.

There is some evidence that certain chemicals, such as fluoride and chlorine, found in the tap water of most

municipalities may not be healthy for dogs, especially smaller dogs like Bostons. In addition, some older homes contain lead pipes, which can add lead to the tap water, and this lead is clearly harmful to dogs. If this matter concerns you, consider using bottled or filtered water for your Boston. For several years, I have used a filtration system, which sits on my kitchen counter, to purify tap water for myself and my dogs. I don't have any scientific proof that it has helped improve the health of my dogs, but I have seen improvements that I think can be attributed to the use of the filtered water.

It is essential that your Boston Terrier have plenty of drinking water available at all times.

I also have a small water bottle with a built-in filter that I take when I travel so that I can provide filtered water for my dogs. This is important because changes in water during travel can cause stomach upset and diarrhea. Rather than carry bottled water with me, as so many dog owners do, I take my filter bottle, fill it with tap water, and use that filtered water to fill my dogs' bowl.

Feeding and Behavior Problems

Occasionally a dog will develop the bad habit of guarding his food. He may growl at anyone who approaches while he is eating, and in extreme cases may snap at people or other dogs who enter the room while he is eating. Food guarding is a natural, instinctive behavior in dogs, in which the strongest member of the pack will not allow weaker pack members to eat until he is finished. In homes where two or more dogs reside, this behavior among the dogs can and does take place with little or no resulting problem. However, if this behavior is leading to bloodshed among your dogs, or if this behavior is being directed at the human pack members (particularly children), it is a serious problem.

One way to manage this problem is to feed your dog in his crate with the door latched. This technique gives him the privacy he needs while he is eating. It does not, however, solve the problem, and it could put someone in danger if at any time the person were to try to take food away from such a dog.

> ### HOW MANY MEALS A DAY?
>
> Individual dogs vary in how much they should eat to maintain a desired body weight—not too fat but not too thin. Puppies need several meals a day, whereas older dogs may need only one. Determine how much food keeps your adult dog looking and feeling his best. Then decide how many meals you want to feed with that amount. Like us, most dogs love to eat, and offering two meals a day is more enjoyable for them. If you're worried about overfeeding, make sure you measure correctly and abstain from adding tidbits to the meals.
>
> Whether you feed one or two meals, leave your dog's food out only for the amount of time it takes him to eat it—10 minutes, for example. *Free-feeding* (when food is available all the time) and leisurely meals encourage picky eating. Don't worry if your dog doesn't finish all of his dinner in the allotted time. He'll learn that he should.

An Ounce of Prevention

You can prevent such problems from arising in the first place by feeding your Boston regular meals and asking him to obey a command, such as sit, before he receives each meal. You can also feed his meals by hand occasionally (more frequently at first), having him earn every bite with a command or trick. In this way, your Boston will learn that you provide all food and are therefore "stronger" than he is. Every human member of the family should participate in feeding your Boston this way, with strict supervision and assistance for young children.

If your Boston Terrier tends to guard his food bowl, simple training techniques can alter the behavior.

SOLVING THE PROBLEM

If your Boston is already guarding his food, you should still feed from the bowl or by hand as a reward for compliance with commands. Teach your Boston the "Off" and "Take It" exercises described in Chapter 8. These exercises will help you teach some other games to your dog that will convince him that great things happen when you are near his food dish.

Never take his food away from him. This action will only convince him that he was right and that he must guard his food more carefully. Instead, be sure that every time you are near his bowl something wonderful appears in it, like a biscuit, a tiny piece of freeze-dried liver or a sliver of grilled steak. If there are kids in the household, save extra-special treats to appear in the bowl when the kids are nearby.

Another helpful technique is to feed him as usual but feed only one or two pieces of kibble or food at a time, walking away as he eats. Return to pick up and refill the dish with one or two more pieces every time he empties it. This action is designed to make your dog want you nearby as he eats.

A variation is to divide your dog's meal in fourths, putting one fourth in the bowl at a time and asking him to comply with your command of sit or lie down (or a trick) before you place the bowl on the floor. By dividing the meal in fourths, your dog has three extra opportunities at each meal to practice obedience around the food bowl. Once your dog is comfortable with this practice and has a very good response to "Sit," you can try interrupting him while he is eating by asking him to sit for a sliver of steak or liver.

Even if your dog does not guard his food dish, it is a good idea to feed him by hand, divide his meals and teach him to comply with commands to earn his meals. These techniques will prevent problems from ever arising during mealtime. If you follow these suggestions and still have behavior problems with your dog during meals, please consult a professional trainer skilled in solving these problems. You can find a good trainer by contacting the Association of Pet Dog Trainers (see Chapter 3).

Resources

BOOKS

Martin, Ann N. *Food Pets Die For.* Troutdale, OR: Newsage Press, 1997.

McKay, Pat. *Reigning Cats and Dogs.* South Pasadena: Oscar Publications, 1992.

Palika, Liz. *The Consumer's Guide to Dog Food.* New York: Howell Book House, 1996.

Pitcairn, Dr. Richard, and Dr. Susan Hubble Pitcairn. *Pitcairn's Complete Guide to Natural Health for Dogs and Cats.* 2d ed. Emmaus, Pa.: Rodale Press, 1995.

Schultze, Kymythy R. *The Ultimate Diet: Natural Nutrition for Dogs and Cats.* Descanso, Calif: Affenbar Ink, 1998.

WEB SITES

Animal Protection Institute. *What's Really in Pet Food.* www.api4animals.org/petfood.htm.

Wolfe, Earl. *Dog Food Comparison Charts.* http://home. hawaii.rr.com/wolfepack/food.html. This Web site lists ingredients of all brands of dog foods.

Grooming

Your

Boston Terrier

Bostons are one of the easier breeds to groom and maintain. Their short coats do shed; however, without the soft undercoats that some breeds have, shedding is minimal. In fact, a healthy Boston should not shed heavily or show excessive hair loss.

Regular Maintenance

Weekly brushing with a soft-bristle palm brush or glove will remove dust, dirt and dead hair, leaving your dog's coat shiny and clean. Regular brushing also promotes healthy skin and coat, stimulating blood flow near the skin surface and promoting normal production of natural oils to protect the coat. Although your Boston's grooming needs are minimal, regular brushing, teeth cleaning and nail trimming will keep her looking handsome and dapper and will give you an opportunity to notice physical changes that might require veterinary attention. In addition, you also will be able to notice skin parasites and pests, such as fleas, before they become a major problem. Please refer to Chapter 7 for details on keeping your Boston Terrier flea-free and in good health.

As you brush her coat, notice her hair: Does it look shiny and healthy, or dull and brittle? Is a small amount of dead hair being shed, or does she seem to be losing a lot of hair? Do you see any bare patches of skin, or lumps or wounds on the skin? Does her skin have a bad odor? Check your Boston Terrier's ears. If they smell musty or yeasty, or really foul, she has a health problem requiring veterinary attention. Likewise, get to know the inside of your Boston Terrier's mouth as you clean her teeth. This places you in the best position to notice abnormalities or changes in your dog's mouth that might require veterinary treatment.

Placing your Boston on a tabletop makes grooming sessions easier for both of you.

Choose the Best Workspace

Grooming is best done on a table or counter covered with a nonslip surface, such as a rubber bath mat. If you have more than one dog, you may want to invest in a grooming table that folds away for storage and has a permanent nonslip surface.

Lay out all of your tools and supplies before you put your dog on the table, and be sure everything is within easy reach. You never want to turn your back and leave her on the table or counter, lest she jump or fall off.

The Grooming Process

A well-groomed dog is a dog that is well looked after. Like humans, dogs need regular and periodic personal care in order to remain at their most attractive and to prevent health problems due to poor grooming, or no grooming. When you give your dog regular and thorough grooming, you are returning the devotion that your dog gives to you.

NAIL TRIMMING

Start by trimming your dog's nails. Gently hold one of her paws in your hand, being very careful not to stretch her leg at an unnatural angle. The closer to her body you hold her paw, the less she will resist nail trimming. One at a time, hold each toe between your thumb and forefinger to give you the best view of the toenail. If it is white or clear, you will be able to see the pink vein, or *quick,* inside the nail. Position the nail clippers at an angle on the toenail to remove the tip of the nail without cutting into the quick.

If you begin clipping her nails while she is still a puppy, your Boston will tolerate the clipping as an adult.

If your dog has some clear nails and some black nails, use the clear nails as a guide to judge how far to cut the black nails in order to avoid cutting the quick. If you do cut the quick, calmly and gently apply a small amount of styptic powder or flour to the bleeding nail, checking after a few moments to be sure the bleeding has stopped. If your dog seems upset, offer a small treat to help her forget the unpleasantness.

Most Boston Terrier breeders have their puppies' dewclaws removed by a veterinarian before the age of 10 days. However, if your dog has dewclaws, check them frequently for excessive length. Because they don't touch the ground, they can grow long enough to curl back and embed in the toe, even when her other toenails are short. The embedded nail can cause pain and infection. If a dewclaw does reach that length, it is best to have your veterinarian examine the paw and cut back the nail for you.

Some Bostons need their nails trimmed every three to four weeks; others require weekly or even semiweekly touchups. You will want to watch the growth of your own dog's nails to determine the best interval for keeping them trimmed. Ideally, the nails should be kept short enough that they don't tap on a hard floor as your dog walks. They most certainly should not grow long enough to cause splaying or displacement of her toes.

> ### QUICK AND PAINLESS NAIL CLIPPING
>
> For quick and painless nail clipping, make a habit of handling your dog's feet and giving treats as you do. When it's time to clip nails, go through the same routine, but take your clippers and snip off just the end of the nail—clip too far down and you'll cut into the *quick*, the nerve center, hurting your dog and causing the nail to bleed. Clip two nails a session while you're getting your dog used to the procedure. Soon you'll be doing all four feet quickly and easily.

GRINDING OR FILING THE NAILS

Some people like to use a cordless nail grinder to smooth the rough edges left by nail clippers. This tool, available from some pet supply retailers, has an abrasive tip that spins at high speed. The tip leaves a smooth edge, but if too much pressure is applied or if it is held on the nail too long, it can grind down to the quick, causing the dog some pain. Breeders who show their dogs often accustom their puppies to the nail grinder before the pups go to their new homes, making the owner's job easier.

If your dog has difficulty allowing you to trim her nails, work with her gently and patiently to teach her to cooperate with you. Look for more details on this subject in "Husbandry Training," found later in this chapter.

TRIMMING HAIR ON THE PAWS

Some Bostons have a great deal of hair between the pads of their paws, which can grow over the pads and cause them to slip when walking on smooth flooring. If this is the case with your Boston, you can use blunt-tipped safety scissors (the type used to trim human infants' fingernails) to carefully trim the excess hair on the bottom of her paws. Be very careful not to pinch or cut her paws while trimming.

EAR CLEANING

The Boston Terrier has naturally erect ears that are less vulnerable to infection than the flopped or folded ears of some other breeds. However, if your dog plays or walks in an area with heavy underbrush, you'll want to check her ears regularly to be sure nothing has fallen into them. A healthy Boston's ears should be clean and odorfree. Regular cleaning with a product designed for that purpose (purchased from your veterinarian or a pet supply retailer) and cotton balls or gauze squares will help you assess your dog's ear health.

GROOMING TOOLS

Pin brush

Slicker brush

Flea comb

Towel

Mat rake

Grooming glove

Scissors

Nail clippers

Tooth-cleaning equipment

Shampoo

Conditioner

Clippers

First, look in the ears. Do they look clean? Do you see any black or brown wax in the ears? Next, smell the ears. Is there a strong odor of any kind? If so, you will want to schedule an appointment with your veterinarian to diagnose the cause.

Then, following the directions on the ear cleaning product you have purchased, squeeze a small amount either directly into the ear canal or onto a cotton ball or gauze pad. If directly into the ear, gently massage the ear to work the solution around before allowing the dog to shake her head. This shaking should eject all of the solution plus any dirt or debris from the ear canal. Gently wipe around the inside of the ear with the cotton balls or gauze pads. Use a clean cotton ball for each ear so that you don't spread a possible infection in one ear to the other ear. Always wipe gently and avoid going very deeply into the ear canal. The action of the dog shaking her head should bring most of the dirt and debris up to the opening where it can be easily wiped away.

Now is a good time to incorporate teeth cleaning into the grooming process. Follow your veterinarian's recommendations for best results. Some people use a soft toothbrush; others prefer the plastic fingertip brush. Still others use a clean gauze square. Whichever tool you select, be sure to use a toothpaste made specifically for dogs. Human toothpaste foams much more than canine toothpaste and can make your Boston sick if she swallows it.

Use a gentle motion to clean away food and other debris and to massage the gums. When you take your Boston in for a health checkup, ask the veterinarian or one of the vet assistants to teach you the best technique for brushing her teeth.

Dental hygiene is important to your Boston Terrier's health.

Bathing Your Boston Terrier

If you are planning to bathe your Boston during a grooming session, first brush the coat to remove dead hair and loose dirt. Prepare your bathing area as you did your grooming area, laying out towels, shampoo and other necessities within easy reach. Most Bostons are small enough to fit in a laundry sink or tub, or the kitchen sink. If not, a bathtub or shower enclosure makes a good bathing area. Be sure the surface of the sink or tub is not slick and gives a solid footing for your dog. The more secure she feels about that, the less anxious she will be about the whole bathing process.

When bathing your Boston, make sure that any shampoos and conditioners you use are made specifically for dogs. Do not use any human shampoos or conditioners unless specifically told to do so by your vet for some medical reason. The normal pH of your dog's skin is different from that of human skin. Using human products may dry your dog's skin and irritate it.

Turn on the water and check it before putting your dog in the tub. It should feel slightly warm, neither hot nor cold. Place your Boston in the tub and apply a small drop of mineral oil or protective eye ointment (available from veterinary ophthalmologists) to each eye. Gently wet her down all over, taking care not to squirt water directly into her ears, eyes or nose. Apply a small amount of dog shampoo, and work it into a good lather all over her body. To wash her face, apply a little bit of shampoo to the top of her head, work it into a lather, and gently move the lather down onto her face, rubbing it in. Do your best to avoid getting shampoo in her eyes.

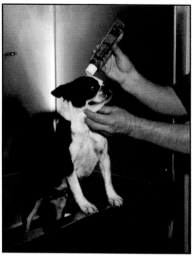

When shampooing your Boston, it is best to use a formula that is specially made for dogs.

Rinse off the shampoo gently and thoroughly with tepid water. You may repeat the shampoo process if she is particularly dirty, but be sure to rinse off every speck of shampoo before proceeding to the next step. Shampoo left in the coat can cause dry skin and itching. If you are using a coat conditioner or creme rinse, follow the label directions exactly, making sure that you completely rinse that product out of the coat as well.

Finally, you are ready to wrap your Boston in a towel and rub her down to dry her hair and skin. Allow her to shake her body if she wishes, because that will remove a great deal of water from her coat. Unless the weather is extremely cold and she must go outside, a hair dryer is unnecessary. The Boston's short single coat usually dries very quickly on its own in the air. Congratulations! You have completed your Boston's grooming.

HOW OFTEN?

The rule for bathing is to do it as often as the dog needs it. If your dog goes swimming or romps in the mud, or rolls in something particularly stinky, it is time for a bath. A healthy Boston who doesn't tend to get dirty playing outside may require a bath only every three to four months. Too-frequent bathing can strip the fur of its natural oils and dry the skin. If you find that your Boston requires bathing at more-frequent intervals because of bad odor or skin irritation, you'll want to consult your veterinarian. Most veterinarians will tell you that if you suspect a skin problem, you should not bathe the dog before the exam.

Husbandry Training

Far too often, grooming becomes an unpleasant chore or a wrestling match between dog and owner. This need not happen to you and your Boston. Some zoos and marine mammal parks have developed "husbandry training." The animals are trained to cooperate with grooming, maintenance, health exams and treatment. Bull elephants have been trained to stand still voluntarily for a foot trim, without restraint. Diabetic monkeys have been trained to extend their arms for blood tests and insulin injections, without restraint. Killer whales have been trained to extend a fin for blood tests and to give a urine sample, all without restraint. If these animals can learn to cooperate, so can your Boston!

Your Boston probably won't need a bath more frequently than once every three to four months, unless she loves rolling around in malodorous messes!

Training a puppy who hasn't had unpleasant experiences with nail trimming or grooming is fairly easy, but any dog can be trained to cooperate with grooming and bathing. Most breeders will trim puppies' nails several times before they leave for their new homes. One hopes that this is a pleasant experience for the pups!

HANDLING DURING MEALS

You will want to spend a few minutes every day for several weeks doing husbandry training. The training is best done during one of your puppy's regular meals. Rather than feeding that meal in a bowl on the floor, place your Boston on the grooming table or counter and feed a few bites of her meal from your hand, while you praise her and tell her what a very wonderful puppy she is. Gently handle her body, one part at a time. As long as she is calm and cooperative, you continue to praise her happily and feed her bites of her meal from your hand. Handle her ears, her head, neck, shoulders, front legs and paws. As each part is handled, praise and feed for calm behavior.

Mealtime can become training time to help your Boston adjust to her grooming sessions.

Cover her eyes for a moment, and praise and feed. Stick a finger in her mouth; praise and feed. Handle her loin, pelvis, tail and hind legs. Handle her chest, abdomen and groin area. Gently pick up each paw in turn and handle it, praising and feeding. Handle the toes, mimicking nail trimming with your fingers, praising and feeding. If at any point during this process your Boston draws away or resists, stop, back up to a part of her body where she enjoyed the handling, and praise and feed for handling that part. Your objective is to make handling a pleasant experience for your Boston and to reassure her that puppy torture is not your objective.

After a few meal/grooming sessions, you will probably find that you can actually trim a toenail without a struggle, praising and feeding her, of course. Likewise, you should be able to gently rub the inside of her ears with a cotton ball, and praise and feed. Before long your Boston should not only cooperate with grooming, but look forward to getting on the grooming table.

Rub-a-Dub-Dub, Train for the Tub

Don't forget about the bathtub! Take a moment to place your puppy in the tub without the water running, and praise and feed her when she relaxes and doesn't struggle to get out. Gradually work up to having the water running and then to spraying her with it, praising and feeding for calm, accepting behavior.

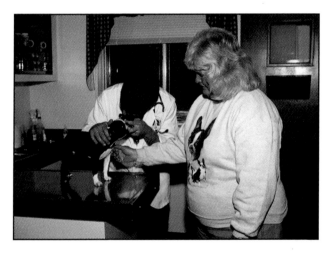

A puppy who gets used to grooming sessions early makes a better patient at the vet's office.

A few minutes a day spent in this way for several weeks will lead to years of happy cooperation during grooming and bathing—and to a better relationship with your dog. An added bonus for your veterinarian is that the dog who relaxes and allows herself to be groomed will also be easier for the vet to examine and treat.

Keeping Your Boston Terrier Healthy

Finding a Veterinarian

Before you bring your Boston Terrier home, select a veterinarian. That way, you can make an appointment for an exam within a few days after getting your dog. Talk to your dog-owning friends and neighbors about their vets. If your puppy's breeder lives in your area, ask for a recommendation. Check with the Boston Terrier rescue program in your area to learn which vets they recommend and why.

An Ounce of Prevention

Good health begins with the selection of a healthy pet. Once you have your Boston, you will want to maintain your dog in the best of health. Good nutrition (see Chapter 5) has a major influence on your dog's health. Vaccinations can help protect your dog from some dangerous diseases. Regular grooming sessions (see Chapter 6), during which you check the condition of his skin, ears and eyes, offer good opportunities to notice any changes in your Boston's condition.

Annual veterinary exams can help you identify and treat health problems before they become serious. If you suspect a health problem, consult your vet promptly. Keeping your Boston and his environment clean and free of pests will also help prevent potentially serious health problems.

Check your dog's teeth frequently and brush them regularly.

Start with your Boston's initial health exam. Make an appointment within a few days of bringing him home. On the day of the appointment, collect a small sample of your dog's feces in a plastic bag to take with you to the vet. Microscopic examination of a fecal sample will tell your vet whether your dog has any intestinal parasites or bacteria. Your vet will also listen to your dog's heart and lungs, look at his eyes and in his ears, take his temperature and check his teeth. This is a good time to ask your vet any questions you might have about your dog's health. If your Boston is due for any vaccinations, your vet will administer them during this exam, provided your dog is in good health.

Vaccinations

Over the years, vaccines have been developed to protect dogs from some very dangerous and even deadly diseases, including distemper, parvovirus and rabies.

Although vaccines certainly do help protect dogs from deadly diseases, don't make the mistake of assuming that vaccines themselves are perfectly safe or harmless. Nor are vaccines 100 percent effective. Occasionally a dog does not develop the proper immunity, and it is possible, though uncommon, for a dog to get a disease even though he has been vaccinated against it.

It is also possible for vaccines to lead to other health problems called vaccine reactions, or *vaccinosis*. Such reactions include *anaphylaxis,* an allergic reaction characterized by swelling and hives that occur a few minutes after the injection. Other adverse reactions, which can happen anytime from immediately after the vaccination to several months later, can include seizures, runny eyes, skin allergies and chronic diarrhea or vomiting.

These conditions are not usually life-threatening but can be a problem for the dog and owner. Conventional medicine has little to offer to cure these chronic problems, which may worsen if the dog is vaccinated again. Holistic medicine, particularly homeopathy, can offer successful treatment for these types of problems. If your Boston develops a chronic problem such as those I have mentioned, you may want to consult a vet trained in the practice of homeopathy (discussed later in this chapter). If you are concerned about adverse reactions to vaccines, it is a good idea to talk to your vet about ways to reduce the risk without increasing your dog's risk of acquiring a disease such as distemper.

YOUR PUPPY'S VACCINES

Vaccines prevent your dog from getting infectious diseases like canine distemper or rabies. Vaccines are the ultimate preventive medicine: They're given before your dog ever gets the disease so that he is protected against it. That's why it is important to have your dog vaccinated routinely. Puppy vaccines start at 8 weeks of age for the five-in-one DHLPP vaccine and are given every three to four weeks until the puppy is 16 months old. Your veterinarian will put your puppy on a proper schedule and will remind you when to bring in your dog for shots.

WEIGHT CONTROL

Like humans, some dogs tend to be more sedentary and to gain weight, whereas others are naturally more active and need to consume more calories to maintain proper weight. These tendencies can vary with age, so a Boston who has been slim all his life can develop a weight gain in older age. Puppies all seem to go through awkward developmental stages during which they look skinny or gangly and can't seem to keep weight on. These conditions usually pass with the dog's growth to maturity.

Is My Dog Too Fat or Too Thin?

The best way to determine whether your Boston is too fat or too thin is to examine him. Can you see every rib and every bone in his spine? If so, he could stand to gain a little weight. Can you feel each rib as you move your hands along his sides? If you can feel, but not see, the ribs, your dog is within his ideal weight range. But, if you cannot feel his ribs, he could stand to lose a few pounds. If you are not sure about your dog's weight, ask your vet.

Consult your veterinarian for safe alternatives to the usual vaccination schedule.

EXERCISE

Bostons do not have special requirements for exercise. A relaxing walk or a few minutes spent chasing a ball or Frisbee in a fenced yard should be sufficient daily exercise. An overweight sedentary Boston should not suddenly begin a vigorous exercise program. Start with short, gentle walks, and gradually increase the distance and the pace as long as he can keep up with you.

SANITATION

Keeping your dog clean is covered in Chapter 6. Keeping your dog's environment clean will help promote good health. Scooping after your dog defecates, whether in your backyard or out on public grounds, helps promote a healthy environment. It reduces the interest that pests, such as flies, slugs, bees and rats, will have in your yard and the surrounding area.

PEST CONTROL

The good news about pest control and Bostons is that it is not that difficult. The Boston's short hair makes your job much easier, in terms of seeing and removing fleas and ticks from his body. If you suspect that your Boston has a parasite problem, consult your vet for advice on the latest developments in products to control fleas and ticks in the environment and on your Boston.

Fleas

Fleas are tiny insects that live in the environment and feed on blood from dogs, cats, humans and other mammals. They do not have wings but are capable of hopping relatively great distances. They hop onto the host to have a meal and then hop off to sleep and lay eggs. Their bites usually cause small red welts, which may itch. Dogs will sometimes scratch at the site of the flea bites. Frequently, the itching centers around the base of the tail, regardless of where on the body the dog is bitten. Many dogs will chew on the base of their tails, creating a *hot spot,* where the hair is pulled or chewed out and the skin underneath is inflamed and moist.

Bostons do not have special exercise needs. A good daily walk is sufficient for him and will do you good, as well.

If you notice these sorts of behaviors, it's time to pull out the flea comb you bought with the rest of your grooming supplies. This very fine-toothed comb will catch fleas in its teeth when you run it through your Boston's hair. Start at his neck, combing toward his tail, and gradually work your way around his body and down his back. When you do catch fleas, quickly dip the comb in a bowl of soapy water, stirring with the comb to dislodge the fleas. This is the quickest, safest, simplest, least expensive method for removing fleas from your dog. You can also bathe your dog in regular dog shampoo, which will drown and wash away any fleas that might be on your dog's body.

In addition to causing itching and allergic reactions, fleas carry tapeworm eggs. These can be transferred to the digestive system of the dog on which the flea feeds if the dog ingests the flea while grooming, licking or chewing on himself in response to the itching.

Humans can become infected with tapeworms in the same manner, so it is important to keep your flea comb away from food preparation or food serving areas (keep it off the kitchen counters and dining tables). After using the flea comb on your dog, wash your hands thoroughly before eating or preparing food.

Flea control is a battle fought on two fronts: your dog and the environment. For your dog, commercial products for flea control include shampoos, dips, sprays, collars, drops and once-a-month oral medication. Regardless of whether the product you choose is labeled as "natural," keep in mind that all these products do contain ingredients that can be toxic to animals and humans, just as they are toxic to fleas and other insects. Consult your vet for recommendations, read all product labels carefully and take product warnings or caution statements very seriously.

These specks in your dog's fur mean he has fleas.

It's not enough to control fleas on your Boston. You must also control fleas in the environment. As mentioned earlier, fleas hop onto the host to have a meal and then hop off again to rest and lay eggs. At any given time, 80 to 90 percent of the overall flea population in your home is not on your dog at all, but in carpets and chair cushions, between floor boards and in other hiding places. Making the environment inhospitable and even toxic to fleas is a very important key to eradicating fleas. Bear in mind that pesticides are, by definition, *toxic,* so consult your vet for recommendations. Read all labels on flea control products, and take any product warning or caution statements very seriously.

FLEAS AND TICKS

There are so many safe, effective products available now to combat fleas and ticks that—thankfully— these pests are less of a problem. Prevention is key, however. Ask your veterinarian about starting your puppy on a flea/tick repellent right away. By combining the use of flea repellent with regular grooming and environmental controls, your dog and your home should stay pestfree. Without this attention, you risk infesting your dog and your home, and you're in for an ugly and costly battle to clear up the problem.

Frequent vacuuming of carpets, floors and furniture helps remove fleas, eggs and larvae from those areas. Dispose of the vacuum-cleaner bag after each use, even if it is not full. Avoid placing anything inside the vacuum-cleaner bag to kill the fleas, such as a flea collar or spray, because the chemicals in the product will be released into the air during vacuuming and can be quite toxic to humans, dogs and other pets.

Birth control pills for fleas? The once-a-month "flea pill" known as *Program* (also a part of the Sentinel product for heartworm and flea prevention) is given to the dog, but it is actually an environmental control product. This product, released into the dog's bloodstream but not metabolized by the dog, renders infertile any fleas that bite the dog. This means that the fleas that bite a dog who has taken Program cannot lay thousands more eggs to make more fleas. Although this measure does not result in instantaneous eradication of fleas, it does have very long-lasting effects on the environment, with little risk to the dog, other pets or humans.

Use tweezers to remove ticks from your dog.

Ticks

Ticks are small insects that usually live outdoors in shrubbery, woods or tall grass. They feed on blood from warm-blooded mammals, including dogs and humans. When a tick bites its host, it burrows its head into the skin, becoming firmly attached to the host. Once the tick has eaten its meal, it withdraws its head from the skin of the host and falls off to crawl away and nest.

In addition to causing an itchy red welt at the site of the bite, ticks can carry some very dangerous diseases. The most well-known is Lyme disease, which can cause flu-like symptoms and joint pain in dogs and humans. Lyme disease is usually successfully treated with antibiotics or homeopathy, although complications can develop in unusual cases. Ticks can also carry Rocky Mountain Spotted Fever, another disease that is usually treated successfully if it is correctly diagnosed.

Heartworm

Heartworm is a parasite that develops in the bloodstream of dogs and is carried by mosquitoes from one dog to another as a microscopic larva. In its mature form, it is a large worm that burrows into the dog's heart, obstructing the blood flow and causing coughing and shortness of breath. This advanced condition is very serious and may be life-threatening. Vets treat heartworm by using extremely toxic substances to kill the worms. The treatment itself can make a dog that is already sick much worse.

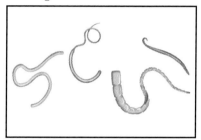

Common internal parasites (l-r): roundworm, whipworm, tapeworm and hookworm.

Prevention is key in dealing with heartworms. Strong, healthy dogs will have more natural resistance to heartworms, and some dogs develop an immunity to them. But by far the safest course is to use the oral medication that your vet can prescribe. Given daily or monthly, according to package directions, this medication controls the microscopic larvae, preventing them from being transmitted from one dog to another via mosquitoes and from becoming the large worms that invade the heart.

Intestinal Parasites

The most common intestinal parasites are roundworms, hookworms, whipworms and tapeworms. These worms live in the digestive tract of dogs, where some feed on nutrients being absorbed into the intestinal walls and others feed on the dog's blood, through the intestinal wall. Except for tapeworms, these parasites are usually spread through feces. When an infected dog defecates on the ground, the feces contain the parasite eggs. Dogs become infected by eating the feces containing the eggs, stepping in it and licking their paws, or walking on soil that has been contaminated by infected feces and licking their paws.

Once a diagnosis is made, your vet can dispense or administer the appropriate medication to kill and remove the worms. Some of the monthly heartworm preventives also have components that help prevent infection from roundworms, hookworms and whipworms. In the case of tapeworms, controlling fleas in the dog's environment will help prevent infestation.

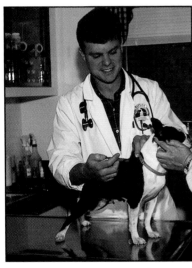

It Runs in the Family

Every breed has its own list of breed-specific problems, and Boston Terriers are no different. However, with proper care, many problems can be averted. Every breed is subject to health problems that are inherited (genetic) or congenital (present at birth but not necessarily genetic). Bostons have their share of problems—not as many as some other breeds but a few more than others. Responsible breeders are

A good relationship with your vet is your first defense when it comes to your dog's health.

aware of these problems and are doing what they can to prevent them from occurring. Dogs that are affected with genetic health problems should not be bred and are usually removed from breeding programs. However, even healthy parents can produce puppies with genetic or environmentally induced congenital defects.

LUXATING PATELLAS

Perhaps the most common genetic problem I have seen in Bostons is *luxating patellas* (also called *slipped stifles*). This is a defect in the shape of the bones of the hind legs where the kneecap, or *patella,* rests in the grooves of the leg bones. The condition usually leads to a dislocation of the kneecap during walking, running or playing. Often the kneecap can slide back in place on its own, and some affected dogs develop the knack of stretching their leg out in such a way that the kneecap slips back into place.

Being small dogs, Bostons are usually able to compensate for this problem by carrying more of their weight on their forelegs when they stand or walk, but the problem can lead to chronic pain and crippling debility. Surgery can correct the defect and anchor the kneecap or the stifle to keep it from slipping out of place. To prevent this problem from occurring, breeders can have their vets examine any dog they are planning to breed, and the vet can establish that the dog has normal patellas. This information can be registered with the Orthopedic Foundation of America (OFA), although such registration is optional.

JUVENILE CATARACTS

Another major congenital problem with Bostons is *juvenile cataracts*. This condition occurs in very young dogs and causes the lens of the eye to become opaque, making the puppy blind at a few months old. Some experts consider juvenile cataracts a common genetic problem, although some cases are reported to be caused by poor nutrition in bottle-fed puppies.

Surgery by a veterinary ophthalmologist can be performed to remove the lens and to allow the dog enough vision to get along. To prevent this problem, breeders can have their breeding dogs examined once a year and certified clear of cataracts through the Canine Eye Research Foundation.

Squeeze eye ointment into the lower lid.

OTHER EYE PROBLEMS

Some Bostons have protruding eyes, making them vulnerable to injuries like a scratched cornea. This type of injury can be diagnosed and treated by your regular vet, and it usually will resolve itself in a couple of days. However, you must follow your vet's instructions carefully and return to the vet if the eye gets worse or doesn't improve within twenty-four to forty-eight hours. Without treatment, corneal scratches can ulcerate and worsen very quickly to the point where the dog may lose his eye.

Some Bostons have problems with tear stains or weepy eyes, as do dogs of other breeds. The condition may be caused by allergies, by clogged or blocked tear ducts or by diet. Work with your vet to determine and treat the cause. If left untreated, the condition may cause an infection that might damage the eye.

THYROID

Low-thyroid disorder, or *hypothyroid,* also seems to run in the breed. Symptoms can include symmetrical hair loss, weight gain and aggressive behavior, but there are many other possible symptoms as well. Blood tests have been developed to check the levels of all hormones produced by the thyroid. Conventional treatment involves giving the dog daily doses of thyroid hormone to replace that which the thyroid is not producing. Holistic treatment seeks to boost the function of the thyroid gland so that it will return to normal hormone production.

HEART

Although heart problems are not really common, Bostons can have them. Bostons tend to have a larger heart relative to their size than many other breeds, a fact that can sometimes lead to a misdiagnosis of an enlarged heart. If your vet suspects that your Boston has an enlarged heart, it is a good idea to make an appointment with a veterinary cardiologist for a thorough examination.

Some Boston puppies are born with a defect called *Patent Ductus Arteriosis,* which means that there is an opening in the wall of the heart somewhere between two of the chambers. This defect can be repaired surgically, although some puppies do outgrow the problem.

MY ACHING BACK!

Although back problems are not considered genetic, certain kinds do seem to run in the breed. *Intervertebral Disc Disease* (IVDD) is not uncommon. Experts link this tendency to the genes that control the shape of the muzzle, making it a breed problem, rather than a family problem. Disc herniation or injury can occur at any point in the spine and should be suspected if the dog's neck seems painful or if any of the legs seem to drag or scrape the ground when the dog is walking.

Bostons as a breed tend to have back problems. Your dog may experience them, or he may not. Your veterinarian can suggest several treatments to ease or eliminate your dog's back pain. This Boston experiments with yoga for his aching back!

In severe cases, surgery by an experienced, board-certified surgeon can restore the dog to normal function and eliminate the pain. Other treatments for less severe cases might include steroids given intravenously or orally, or muscle-relaxing drugs. Both are short-term therapies to be used in acute cases. Acupuncture and chiropractic manipulation can help relieve the pain and inflammation of an acute episode, as well as help prevent future acute flareups in dogs having the condition. Treating with acupuncture and chiropractic therapies avoids the side effects of steroid treatment, which can be harmful when used for more than a short time.

Hemivertebra is a malformation of one of the bones of the spine (vertebrae), in which the bone is smaller than normal and oddly shaped. This is not usually considered a problem, as nearly every Boston has at least one hemivertebra in his tail—that is what causes the screw tail! Hemivertebrae can occur in other parts of the spine. Usually there are no outward symptoms. In unusual cases, the bone is so small and misshapen that there is not enough space for the spinal cord to pass through, resulting in pinched nerves, pain and paralysis.

Spondylosis is a spinal disease seen more commonly in older dogs. The bones of the spine become fused and rigid, causing pain that can be severe at times. Spondylosis is commonly treated with anti-inflammatory medications or steroids. Acupuncture and chiropractic manipulation can help reduce the pain and discomfort and restore some flexibility to the spine, improving the dog's mobility.

BREATHING PROBLEMS

Many Bostons do snore because of the configuration of their short muzzles. The snoring is not considered a problem as a rule. However, a few Bostons have mechanical problems that make it more difficult for them to breathe. They may pant more than normal when exercising, or they may breathe very noisily after only a little bit of exertion. Possible causes are *stenotic nares,* extremely narrow nostrils, or an *elongated soft palate,* which hangs down in the throat and obstructs the dog's airway. Both problems can be corrected surgically, and neither one is extremely common in the breed. Stenotic nares can be diagnosed by your regular vet and can probably be corrected at the same time your dog is spayed or neutered. Elongated soft palate is usually best diagnosed with the dog under anesthesia. Most vets do not have extensive experience in correcting this problem surgically, so it is best to consult a surgical specialist or a vet with a great deal of experience in successfully correcting this problem.

Cancer can happen in any breed, but a certain type of cancer, called *Mast cell tumors*, seems more common in Bostons than in some other breeds. This cancer usually appears as a lump or discoloration on the skin, and it usually grows larger, sometimes growing quite quickly.

Usually these tumors are removed surgically and sent to a pathology lab for analysis. The lab report will tell you whether the tumor is cancerous or not, what kind of cancer it is, whether the tumor was completely removed and whether the cancer may have spread to other parts of the body. Frequently, Mast cell tumors are removed from the skin before they have a chance to spread, and no further treatment is needed. Sometimes the pathologist or your vet will recommend follow-up treatment with steroids or other medications that have been shown to help in such cases. If the pathologist indicates that the cancer may have spread, it might be helpful to consult a veterinary oncologist.

Family Planning

You want to enjoy your pet Boston to the fullest, so the best decision is to have your dog spayed or neutered. This will help ensure good health and safety for your dog, and will probably increase his life expectancy.

WHAT ARE WE TALKING ABOUT?

Spay is the commonly used term for *ovarohysterectomy:* the surgical removal of the female dog's ovaries and uterus. This procedure removes the glands and organs responsible for heat cycles, ovulation and

---

ADVANTAGES OF SPAYING/NEUTERING

The greatest advantage of spaying (for females) or neutering (for males) is that you are guaranteed your dog will not produce puppies. Too many puppies are already available for too few homes. There are other advantages as well.

ADVANTAGES OF SPAYING

No messy heats

No "suitors" howling at your windows or waiting in your yard

No risk of *pyometra* (a disease of the uterus) and decreased incidences of mammary cancer

ADVANTAGES OF NEUTERING

Decreased incidences of fighting (but no effect on the dog's personality)

Decreased roaming in search of bitches in season

Decreased incidences of many urogenital diseases

---

pregnancy in the female. Spaying does reduce the level of female hormones in the female dog's system but will not make her more "masculine."

Neuter is the commonly used term for *castration:* the surgical removal of the male dog's testicles. This procedure removes the glands that produce sperm. Neutering does not reduce the amount of the male hormone testosterone in the male dog's system and will not make a male dog more "feminine."

ADVANTAGES OF SPAYING AND NEUTERING

Unspayed females are very vulnerable to several life-threatening health problems that are eliminated or reduced by spaying. These include uterine cancer (risk eliminated), mammary cancer (risk significantly reduced by spaying before first heat cycle) and *pyometra,* a uterine infection that is frequently undetected and undiagnosed until it becomes life-threatening (risk eliminated).

Neutered male dogs are automatically protected from testicular cancer and are less likely to develop prostate cancer later in life. An added advantage is that neutered males are less likely to wander off in search of a female in heat.

Alternatives for Optimal Health

In addition to conventional veterinary treatment for your Boston, most owners now have access to alternative treatments that can be very helpful in relieving pain, curing some illnesses and enhancing the dog's general health and well-being.

ACUPUNCTURE

The practice of inserting very thin, fine needles into specific points, or meridians, on the body has been used in China for thousands of years to relieve pain, cure disease and prevent illness. In the United States, vets certified in acupuncture use it primarily to relieve pain and decrease the effects of chronic disease such as renal failure. Acupuncture is known to reduce inflammation and reduce pain, so it is commonly used to treat arthritis, hip dysplasia, degenerative disc disease and spondylosis.

The International Veterinary Acupuncture Society is the primary source of training and is the organization that certifies veterinary acupuncturists in the United States. You can contact this organization to locate an acupuncturist for your Boston. You will find address information in the "Resources" section at the end of the chapter.

CHIROPRACTIC

Chiropractic is a widely known treatment for spinal problems in humans, and it is becoming more popular for the treatment of animals as well. Certification is available for veterinary chiropractors, who must be licensed vets, though some states allow human chiropractors to be licensed. The classes and certification are offered by the American Veterinary Chiropractic Association. Chiropractic is especially helpful to Bostons, who have a breed predisposition to intervertebral disc disease and to spondylosis.

CHINESE HERBAL MEDICINE

Like acupuncture, Chinese Herbal Medicine (CHM) has been used in China for thousands of years, primarily on humans. Unlike the Western herbal folk medicine most of us are familiar with, CHM views the whole list of symptoms and uses traditional herbal combinations to rebalance the body and eliminate the symptoms. CHM can be used to treat many conditions, including chronic bowel or skin problems, immune deficiencies and behavior problems. Some vets in the United States receive extensive training, spanning several years, in the use of CHM, although no certification is currently available.

You may choose to utilize alternative therapies to maximize your Boston's health.

HOMEOPATHY

Developed about 200 years ago by physician Samuel Hahnemann, homeopathy uses "remedies"—natural substances, in very potent form—to cure disease. Homeopathy has been used successfully in animals and people for first aid and for treatment of long-standing or chronic conditions. It has been helpful in treating skin problems and allergies, irritable bowel, chronic vomiting, kidney and liver problems and a host of other illnesses. Homeopathy is very useful in treating illness brought on by vaccination. A few very skilled veterinary practitioners have had success in treating certain cancers.

WHEN TO SEEK PROFESSIONAL HELP

There are many instances in which it is advisable to seek the help of your veterinarian. In case of emergency, seek professional help if your dog:

Has lacerations that require suturing or has a broken bone requiring splinting or surgery.

Loses consciousness for any reason.

Is bleeding and you cannot stop it with pressure.

Is bleeding from the mouth, nose, ear or rectum.

Has pain that causes him to cry out or behave aggressively.

Has a high fever.

Has ingested a poisonous substance.

Is vomiting excessively or has uncontrolled or bloody diarrhea.

Has any type of eye injury.

Suddenly becomes extremely lethargic and difficult to rouse.

Has difficulty breathing.

Has pale or blue gums.

HERBAL MEDICINE

Traditional herbal medicine involves the use of certain herbs to treat specific symptoms. Many conventional medications are based on herbal remedies. This form of treatment can be very helpful in treating isolated conditions or in relieving symptoms.

In using herbs for medicinal use, take care to avoid combining herbs that might create an adverse reaction. It is a good idea to consult with an experienced practitioner and make certain that you have a reliable diagnosis before beginning treatment. To learn more about herbal medicine, consult some of the books listed in the "Resources" section at the end of this chapter.

SOFT TISSUE MASSAGE

Massage therapy has long been used to give pain relief, relax stiff or sore muscles, and reduce muscle spasms.

Some human massage therapists have studied canine anatomy and physiology and offer professional services for dogs and cats. There are also some books and videos that can help you learn to massage your Boston safely and comfortably at home.

In Case of Emergency

Despite your best efforts to keep your Boston safe from harm, accidents and emergencies can happen. Being prepared could make a big difference in the outcome.

First, keep your vet's telephone number handy so that you can call in an emergency. Talk to your vet before any emergency arises about his or her recommendations for what you should do. Many of the larger urban centers now have veterinary hospitals that operate after normal office hours to handle emergencies.

> **POISON ALERT**
>
> If your dog has ingested a potentially poisonous substance, waste no time. Call the National Animal Poison Control Center hot line:
>
> **(800) 548-2423**
> ($30 per case)
>
> or
>
> **(900) 680-0000**
> ($20 for first five minutes; $2.95 for each additional minute)

FIRST AID

In addition to important phone numbers, it is a good idea to have a few first aid supplies on hand in case of an emergency. Check with your own vet for his or her recommendations on what your first aid kit should include.

 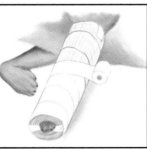

Make a temporary splint by wrapping the leg in firm casing and then bandaging it.

It is important to remember that any dog who is in pain may behave abnormally and might even bite someone trying to help him. Therefore, only do what you can safely do for your dog without the risk of being bitten. Because it is difficult to muzzle a Boston, if your dog truly resists your efforts to help him, handle him very carefully and take him directly to your vet or the emergency facility, where the staff is trained to handle such cases without harming your dog or being bitten.

Use a scarf or old hose to make a temporary muzzle, as shown.

If your dog is bleeding, use gauze pads and wrap to apply pressure directly to the wound in order to stop the bleeding. If you are unable to stop the bleeding in a few minutes, call your vet or the emergency hospital for advice. You may have to take your dog in for treatment. Bleeding from the mouth or rectum may indicate internal injuries. You cannot control this kind of bleeding with first aid, and you must seek professional help as soon as possible.

HEATSTROKE

One of the major dangers facing Bostons is heatstroke. Because of their dark coats and shortened muzzles, they have a greater tendency than other breeds to suffer from the heat and to overheat. *Heatstroke* occurs when the body's ability to release heat cannot keep up with the high temperature of the air around the body. The dog may breathe rapidly or pant loudly. He may become disoriented and stagger, vomit, collapse or have a seizure and then die as his blood cells break down from being cooked, literally.

You can prevent heatstroke by keeping your Boston indoors and cool during warm weather, avoiding hot cars and taking plenty of cool water and ice with you if you must be out and about in warmer weather. Do not leave your Boston unattended in a car; even on a cool day, the sun can warm the temperature inside the car to dangerously high levels. Do not allow your Boston to exercise vigorously or to remain outdoors in extreme heat.

If your Boston overheats, get him to a cool location in shade as quickly as possible. Bathe him in cool (not ice-cold) water and turn a fan on him to evaporate the water and cool his body. Take his temperature with your rectal thermometer. If it is at all higher than normal, continue your attempts to cool him down as you transport him to your veterinarian or the nearest emergency hospital. Usually a vet will start intravenous fluid therapy to cool the body, and the vet may even have to give a blood or plasma transfusion if the heatstroke is in an advanced stage.

Your Boston's Golden Years

As your Boston ages, certain changes will occur in his body. He may develop a tendency to gain weight, or he may lose weight as he ages. Any significant weight change should be discussed with your vet, because it may be a symptom of an underlying problem. Likewise, changes in eating habits or drinking patterns should also be noted and discussed with your vet. Any changes in urination or defecation patterns or habits, such as increased frequency, accidents in the house, or changes in color or texture should also be discussed with your vet.

Older Bostons may develop problems such as old-age cataracts, corneal dystrophy, Cushings disease, diabetes, arthritis or heart disease. Most of these problems are related to advanced age and are not extremely common to the breed.

FIRST AID SUPPLIES

Gauze pads, assorted sizes

Gauze bandage, several widths

Adhesive tape

Cotton balls

Cotton swabs

Ace bandage

Vet wrap

Hydrogen peroxide

Antibiotic ointment or cream

Antibiotic eye ointment or drops

Benadryl, liquid or pills

Isopropyl alcohol

Rectal thermometer and lubricant

Buffered aspirin
(not acetominophen)

Tweezers

Small scissors

Your older dog will probably slow down, requiring less exercise and more sleep than he did when he was a younger adult. It is important to ensure that he gets sufficient exercise without overexerting. He also may become stiff with arthritis or muscle atrophy, both problems of advancing age. As this happens, you can reduce the discomfort with conventional medications or alternative therapies.

Your older dog will continue to be a loyal companion throughout his life.

Be sure that you continue to provide him with plenty of water and a properly balanced diet. If he tends to put on more weight, you can alter the balance in his diet a little by increasing the portion of vegetables or by adding lightly cooked vegetables to his dry food. If he develops an illness that requires a specialized diet, work closely with your vet to ensure that you are meeting your dog's new nutritional needs.

Above all, you want to be sure that this longtime, faithful companion remains in the mainstream of family activity, even though his hair may be gray or thinning and his gait may be a bit stiff or slower. Short, slow walks and gentle play will help keep him in shape.

Saying Good-Bye

Advances in veterinary medicine enable you to maintain a better level of health in your Boston for a longer time than you could have just a few years ago. New pain relievers and treatments for diseases, and newly rediscovered alternatives, such as acupuncture, chiropractic and homeopathy, offer many opportunities to help the older Boston lead a healthier and more comfortable life. At some point, however, the body gives out, medicine no longer relieves symptoms, and pain may be overwhelming. You must then work as a team with your vet and your dog to make those difficult choices that may be the most helpful to your beloved Boston.

EUTHANASIA: THE GOOD SLEEP

Sometimes, perhaps when your pet is in pain that cannot be relieved, you may have to make the difficult decision to help his body let go of life before it is ready. This is something no one ever wants to do, yet it is a decision that must be considered carefully and planned for in advance. Your vet can help you discuss and make arrangements ahead of time, but you will be the one who is best suited to make the final decision. You know your companion better than anyone else, and he will rely on you to help him when he is ready to let go of life.

Resources

BOOKS

Ball, Stefan, and Judy Howard. *Bach Flower Remedies for Pets.* Essex, U.K.: C. W. Daniel, 1999.

Goldstein, Martin, D.V.M. *The Nature of Animal Healing: The Path to Your Pet's Health, Happiness, and Longevity.* New York: Knopf, 1999.

Graham, Helen, and Gregory Vlamis. *Bach Flower Remedies for Pets.* Tallahassee, Fla: Findhorn Press, 1999.

Hourdebaight, Jean Pierre. *Canine Massage.* New York: Howell Book House, 1999.

Pitcairn, Richard, D.V.M., and Susan Hubble Pitcairn. *Dr. Pitcairn's Complete Guide to Natural Health for Dogs and Cats.* 2d ed. Emmaus, Pa: Rodale Press, 1995.

Schwartz, Cheryl, D.V.M. *Four Paws Five Directions: A Guide to Chinese Medicine for Dogs and Cats.* Berkeley, Calif: Celestial Arts Press, 1996.

Tilford, Gregory, and Mary Wulff-Tilford. *Herbs for Pets.* Mission Viejo, CA: Bowtie Press, 1999.

HOLISTIC VETERINARY ASSOCIATIONS

American Holistic Veterinary Medical Association
2214 Old Emmorton Rd.
Bel Air, MD 21014
www.altvetmed.com/AHVMA_brochure.html

American Veterinary Chiropractic Association
623 Main St.
Hillsdale, IL 61257

International Veterinary Acupuncture Society
P.O. Box 1478
Longmont, CO 80502
www.ivas.org

Complementary and Alternative Veterinary Medicine
www.altvetmed.com

Your Happy, Healthy Pet

Your Dog's Name _____

Name on Your Dog's Pedigree (if your dog has one) _____
_____

Where Your Dog Came From _____
_____

Your Dog's Birthday _____

Your Dog's Veterinarian

    Name _____

    Address _____

    Phone Number_____

    Emergency Number_____

Your Dog's Health

    Vaccines

    type _____ date given _____

    type _____ date given _____

    type _____ date given _____

    type _____ date given _____

    Heartworm

    date tested _____ type used_____ start date _____

Your Dog's License Number_____

Groomer's Name and Number _____

Dogsitter/Walker's Name and Number_____

Awards Your Dog Has Won

    Award _____ date earned _____

    Award _____ date earned _____

part three

Enjoying
your
Dog

Basic
Training

by Ian Dunbar, Ph.D., MRCVS

Training is the jewel in the crown—the most important aspect of doggy husbandry. There is no more important variable influencing dog behavior and temperament than the dog's education: A well-trained, well-behaved and good-natured puppydog is always a joy to live with, but an untrained and uncivilized dog can be a perpetual nightmare. Moreover, deny the dog an education and she will not have the opportunity to fulfill her own canine potential; neither will she have the ability to communicate effectively with her human companions.

Luckily, modern psychological training methods are easy, efficient, effective and, above all, considerably dog-friendly and user-friendly.

Doggy education is as simple as it is enjoyable. But before you can have a good time play-training with your new dog, you have to learn what to do and how to do it. There is no bigger variable influencing the success of dog training than the *owner's* experience and expertise. *Before you embark on the dog's education, you must first educate yourself.*

Basic Training for Owners

Ideally, basic owner training should begin well *before* you select your dog. Find out all you can about your chosen breed first, then master rudimentary training and handling skills. If you already have your puppy-dog, owner training is a dire emergency—the clock is ticking! Especially for puppies, the first few weeks at home are the most important and influential days in the dog's life. Indeed, the cause of most adolescent and adult problems may be traced back to the initial days the pup explores her new home. This is the time to establish the *status quo*—to teach the puppydog how you would like her to behave and so prevent otherwise quite predictable problems.

In addition to consulting breeders and breed books such as this one (which understandably have a positive breed bias), seek out as many pet owners with your breed as you can find. Good points are obvious. What you want to find out are the breed-specific *problems,* so you can nip them in the bud. In particular, you should talk to owners with *adolescent* dogs and make a list of all anticipated problems. Most important, *test drive* at least half a dozen adolescent and adult dogs of your breed yourself. An 8-week-old puppy is deceptively easy to handle, but she will acquire adult size, speed and strength in just four months, so you should learn now what to prepare for.

Puppy and pet dog training classes offer a convenient venue to locate pet owners and observe dogs in action. For a list of suitable trainers in your area, contact the Association of Pet Dog Trainers (see chapter 13). You may also begin your basic owner training by observing other owners in class. Watch as many classes and test drive as many dogs as possible. Select an upbeat, dog-friendly, people-friendly, fun-and-games, puppydog pet training class to learn the ropes. Also, watch training videos and read training books. You must find out what to do and how to do it *before* you have to do it.

Principles of Training

Most people think training comprises teaching the dog to do things such as sit, speak and roll over, but even a 4-week-old pup knows how to do these things already. Instead, the first step in training involves teaching the dog human words for each dog behavior and activity and for each aspect of the dog's environment. That way you, the owner, can more easily participate in the dog's domestic education by directing her to perform specific actions appropriately, that is, at the right time, in the right place and so on. Training opens communication channels, enabling an educated dog to at least understand her owner's requests.

In addition to teaching a dog *what* we want her to do, it is also necessary to teach her *why* she should do what we ask. Indeed, 95 percent of training revolves around motivating the dog *to want to do* what we want. Dogs often understand what their owners want; they just don't see the point of doing it—especially when the owner's repetitively boring and seemingly senseless instructions are totally at odds with much more pressing and exciting doggy distractions. It is not so much the dog that is being stubborn or dominant; rather, it is the owner who has failed to acknowledge the dog's needs and feelings and to approach training from the dog's point of view.

THE MEANING OF INSTRUCTIONS

The secret to successful training is learning how to use training lures to predict or prompt specific behaviors—to coax the dog to do what you want *when* you want. Any highly valued object (such as a treat or toy) may be used as a lure, which the dog will follow with her eyes and nose. Moving the lure in specific ways entices the dog to move her nose, head and entire body in specific ways. In fact, by learning the art of manipulating various lures, it is possible to teach the dog to assume virtually any body position and perform any action. Once you have control over the expression of the dog's behaviors and can elicit any body position or behavior at will, you can easily teach the dog to perform on request.

Teach your dog words for each activity she needs to know, like down.

Tell your dog what you want her to do, use a lure to entice her to respond correctly, then profusely praise and maybe reward her once she performs the desired action. For example, verbally request "Tina, sit!" while you move a squeaky toy upwards and backwards over the dog's muzzle (lure-movement and hand signal), smile knowingly as she looks up (to follow the lure) and sits down (as a result of canine anatomical engineering), then praise her to distraction ("Gooood Tina!"). Squeak the toy, offer a training treat and give your dog and yourself a pat on the back.

Being able to elicit desired responses over and over enables the owner to reward the dog over and over. Consequently, the dog begins to think training is fun. For example, the more the dog is rewarded for sitting, the more she enjoys sitting. Eventually the dog comes to realize that, whereas most sitting is appreciated, sitting immediately upon request usually prompts especially enthusiastic praise and a slew of high-level rewards. The dog begins to sit on cue much of the time, showing that she is starting to grasp the meaning of the owner's verbal request and hand signal.

WHY COMPLY?

Most dogs enjoy initial lure-reward training and are only too happy to comply with their owners' wishes. Unfortunately, repetitive drilling without appreciative feedback tends to diminish the dog's enthusiasm until she eventually fails to see the point of complying anymore. Moreover, as the dog approaches adolescence she becomes more easily distracted as she develops other interests. Lengthy sessions with repetitive exercises tend to bore and demotivate both parties. If it's not fun, the owner doesn't do it and neither does the dog.

Integrate training into your dog's life: The greater number of training sessions each day and the *shorter* they are, the more willingly compliant your dog will

become. Make sure to have a short (just a few seconds) training interlude before every enjoyable canine activity. For example, ask your dog to sit to greet people, to sit before you throw her Frisbee and to sit for her supper. Really, sitting is no different from a canine "Please."

To train your dog, you need gentle hands, a loving heart and a good attitude.

Also, include numerous short training interludes during every enjoyable canine pastime, for example, when playing with the dog or when she is running in the park. In this fashion, doggy distractions may be effectively converted into rewards for training. Just as all games have rules, fun becomes training . . . and training becomes fun.

Eventually, rewards actually become unnecessary to continue motivating your dog. If trained with consideration and kindness, performing the desired behaviors will become self-rewarding and, in a sense, your dog will motivate herself. Just as it is not necessary to reward a human companion during an enjoyable walk in the park, or following a game of tennis, it is hardly necessary to reward our best friend—the dog—for walking by our side or while playing fetch. Human company during enjoyable activities is reward enough for most dogs.

Even though your dog has become self-motivating, it's still good to praise and pet her a lot and offer rewards once in a while, especially for a good job well done. And if for no other reason, praising and rewarding others is good for the human heart.

PUNISHMENT

Without a doubt, lure-reward training is by far the best way to teach: Entice your dog to do what you want and then reward her for doing so. Unfortunately, a human shortcoming is to take the good for granted and to moan and groan at the bad. Specifically, the dog's many good behaviors are ignored while the owner focuses on punishing the dog for making mistakes. In extreme cases, instruction is *limited* to punishing mistakes made by a trainee dog, child, employee or husband, even though it has been proven punishment training is notoriously inefficient and ineffective and is decidedly unfriendly and combative. It teaches the dog that training is a drag, almost as quickly as it teaches the dog to dislike her trainer. Why treat our best friends like our worst enemies?

Punishment training is also much more laborious and time consuming. Whereas it takes only a finite amount of time to teach a dog what to chew, for example, it takes much, much longer to punish the dog for each and every mistake. Remember, *there is only one right way!* So why not teach that right way from the outset?!

To make matters worse, punishment training causes severe lapses in the dog's reliability. Since it is obviously impossible to punish the dog each and every time she misbehaves, the dog quickly learns to distinguish between those times when she must comply (so as to avoid impending punishment) and those times when she need not comply, because punishment is impossible. Such times include when the dog is off leash and 6 feet away, when the owner is otherwise engaged (talking to a friend, watching television, taking a shower, tending to the baby or chatting on the telephone) or when the dog is left at home alone.

Instances of misbehavior will be numerous when the owner is away, because even when the dog complied in the owner's looming presence, she did so unwillingly. The dog was forced to act against her will, rather than molding her will to want to please. Hence, when the owner is absent, not only does the dog know she need not comply, she simply does not want to. Again, the trainee is not a stubborn vindictive beast, but rather the trainer has failed to teach. Punishment training invariably creates unpredictable Jekyll and Hyde behavior.

Trainer's Tools

Many training books extol the virtues of a vast array of training paraphernalia and electronic and metallic gizmos, most of which are designed for canine restraint, correction and punishment, rather than for actual facilitation of doggy education. In reality, most effective training tools are not found in stores; they come from within ourselves. In addition to a willing dog, all you really need is a functional human brain, gentle hands, a loving heart and a good attitude.

In terms of equipment, all dogs do require a quality buckle collar to sport dog tags and to attach the leash (for safety and to comply with local leash laws). Hollow chew toys (like Kongs or sterilized longbones) and a dog bed or collapsible crate are musts for housetraining. Three additional tools are required:

1. specific lures (training treats and toys) to predict and prompt specific desired behaviors;

2. rewards (praise, affection, training treats and toys) to reinforce for the dog what a lot of fun it all is; and

3. knowledge—how to convert the dog's favorite activities and games (potential distractions to training) into "life-rewards," which may be employed to facilitate training.

The most powerful of these is *knowledge*. Education is the key! Watch training classes, participate in training classes, watch videos, read books, enjoy play-training with your dog and then your dog will say "Please," and your dog will say "Thank you!"

Housetraining

If dogs were left to their own devices, certainly they would chew, dig and bark for entertainment and then no doubt highlight a few areas of their living space with sprinkles of urine, in much the same way we decorate by hanging pictures. Consequently, when we ask a dog to live with us, we must teach her *where* she may dig, *where* she may perform her toilet duties, *what* she may chew and *when* she may bark. After all, when left at home alone for many hours, we cannot expect the dog to amuse herself by completing crosswords or watching the soaps on TV!

Also, it would be decidedly unfair to keep the house rules a secret from the dog, and then get angry and punish the poor critter for inevitably transgressing rules she did not even know existed. Remember: Without adequate education and guidance, the dog will be forced to establish her own rules—doggy rules—and most probably will be at odds with the owner's view of domestic living.

Since most problems develop during the first few days the dog is at home, prospective dog owners must be certain they are quite clear about the principles of housetraining *before* they get a dog. Early misbehaviors quickly become established as the *status quo*—

becoming firmly entrenched as hard-to-break bad habits, which set the precedent for years to come. Make sure to teach your dog good habits right from the start. Good habits are just as hard to break as bad ones!

Ideally, when a new dog comes home, try to arrange for someone to be present as much as possible during the first few days (for adult dogs) or weeks for puppies. With only a little forethought, it is surprisingly easy to find a puppy sitter, such as a retired person, who would be willing to eat from your refrigerator and watch your television while keeping an eye on the newcomer to encourage the dog to play with chew toys and to ensure she goes outside on a regular basis.

POTTY TRAINING

To teach the dog where to relieve herself:

1. never let her make a single mistake;

2. let her know where you want her to go; and

3. handsomely reward her for doing so: "GOOOOOOOD DOG!!!" liver treat, liver treat, liver treat!

Preventing Mistakes

A single mistake is a training disaster, since it heralds many more in future weeks. And each time the dog soils the house, this further reinforces the dog's unfortunate preference for an indoor, carpeted toilet. *Do not let an unhousetrained dog have full run of the house.*

When you are away from home, or cannot pay full attention, confine the dog to an area where elimination is appropriate, such as an outdoor run or, better still, a small, comfortable indoor kennel with access to an outdoor run. When confined in this manner, most dogs will naturally housetrain themselves.

If that's not possible, confine the dog to an area, such as a utility room, kitchen, basement or garage, where elimination may not be desired in the long run but as an interim measure it is certainly preferable to doing it all around the house. Use newspaper to cover the floor of the dog's day room. The newspaper may be used to soak up the urine and to wrap up and dispose of the feces. Once your dog develops a preferred spot for eliminating, it is only necessary to cover that part of the floor with newspaper. The smaller papered area may then be moved (only a little each day) towards the door to the outside. Thus the dog will develop the tendency to go to the door when she needs to relieve herself.

Never confine an unhousetrained dog to a crate for long periods. Doing so would force the dog to soil the crate and ruin its usefulness as an aid for housetraining (see the following discussion).

Teaching Where

In order to teach your dog where you would like her to do her business, you have to be there to direct the proceedings—an obvious, yet often neglected, fact of life. In order to be there to teach the dog *where* to go, you need to know *when* she needs to go. Indeed, the success of housetraining depends on the owner's ability to predict these times. Certainly, a regular feeding schedule will facilitate prediction somewhat, but there is nothing like "loading the deck" and influencing the timing of the outcome yourself!

Whenever you are at home, make sure the dog is under constant supervision and/or confined to a small

The first few weeks at home are the most important and influential in your dog's life.

107

area. If already well trained, simply instruct the dog to lie down in her bed or basket. Alternatively, confine the dog to a crate (doggy den) or tie-down (a short, 18-inch lead that can be clipped to an eye hook in the baseboard near her bed). Short-term close confinement strongly inhibits urination and defecation, since the dog does not want to soil her sleeping area. Thus, when you release the puppydog each hour, she will definitely need to urinate immediately and defecate every third or fourth hour. Keep the dog confined to her doggy den and take her to her intended toilet area each hour, every hour and on the hour.

When taking your dog outside, instruct her to sit quietly before opening the door—she will soon learn to sit by the door when she needs to go out!

Teaching Why

Being able to predict when the dog needs to go enables the owner to be on the spot to praise and reward the dog. Each hour, hurry the dog to the intended toilet area in the yard, issue the appropriate instruction ("Go pee!" or "Go poop!"), then give the dog three to four minutes to produce. Praise and offer a couple of training treats when successful. The treats are important because many people fail to praise their dogs with feeling . . . and housetraining is hardly the time for understatement. So either loosen up and enthusiastically praise that dog: "Wuzzzer-wuzzer-wuzzer, hoooser good wuffer den? Hoooo went pee for Daddy?" Or say "Good dog!" as best you can and offer the treats for effect.

Following elimination is an ideal time for a spot of play-training in the yard or house. Also, an empty dog may be allowed greater freedom around the house for the next half hour or so, just as long as you keep an eye out to make sure she does not get into other kinds of mischief. If you are preoccupied and cannot pay full attention, confine the dog to her doggy den once more to enjoy a peaceful snooze or to play with her many chew toys.

If your dog does not eliminate within the allotted time outside—no biggie! Back to her doggy den, and then try again after another hour.

As I own large dogs, I always feel more relaxed walking an empty dog, knowing that I will not need to finish our stroll weighted down with bags of feces!

Beware of falling into the trap of walking the dog to get her to eliminate. The good ol' dog walk is such an enormous highlight in the dog's life that it represents the single biggest potential reward in domestic dogdom. However, when in a hurry, or during inclement weather, many owners abruptly terminate the walk the moment the dog has done her business. This, in effect, severely punishes the dog for doing the right thing, in the right place at the right time. Consequently, many dogs become strongly inhibited from eliminating outdoors because they know it will signal an abrupt end to an otherwise thoroughly enjoyable walk.

Instead, instruct the dog to relieve herself in the yard prior to going for a walk. If you follow the above instructions, most dogs soon learn to eliminate on cue. As soon as the dog eliminates, praise (and offer a treat or two)—"Good dog! Let's go walkies!" Use the walk as a reward for eliminating in the yard. If the dog does not go, put her back in her doggy den and think about a walk later on. You will find with a "No feces—no walk" policy, your dog will become one of the fastest defecators in the business.

If you do not have a backyard, instruct the dog to eliminate right outside your front door prior to the walk. Not only will this facilitate clean up and disposal of the feces in your own trash can but, also, the walk may again be used as a colossal reward.

CHEWING AND BARKING

Short-term close confinement also teaches the dog that occasional quiet moments are a reality of domestic living. Your puppydog is extremely impressionable during her first few weeks at home. Regular confinement at this time soon exerts a calming influence over the dog's personality. Remember, once the dog is housetrained and calmer, there will be a whole lifetime ahead for the dog to enjoy full run of the house and garden. On the other hand, by letting the newcomer have unrestricted access to the entire household and allowing her to run willy-nilly, she will most certainly develop a bunch of behavior problems in short order, no doubt necessitating confinement later in life. It would not be fair to remedially restrain and confine a dog you have trained, through neglect, to run free.

When confining the dog, make sure she always has an impressive array of suitable chew toys. Kongs and sterilized longbones (both readily available from pet stores) make the best chew toys, since they are hollow and may be stuffed with treats to heighten the dog's interest. For example, by stuffing the little hole at the top of a Kong with a small piece of freeze-dried liver, the dog will not want to leave it alone.

Remember, treats do not have to be junk food and they certainly should not represent extra calories. Rather, treats should be part of each dog's regular

daily diet: Some food may be served in the dog's bowl for breakfast and dinner, some food may be used as training treats, and some food may be used for stuffing chew toys. I regularly stuff my dogs' many Kongs with different shaped biscuits and kibble.

Make sure your puppy has suitable chew toys.

The kibble seems to fall out fairly easily, as do the oval-shaped biscuits, thus rewarding the dog instantaneously for checking out the chew toys. The bone-shaped biscuits fall out after a while, rewarding the dog for worrying at the chew toy. But the triangular biscuits never come out. They remain inside the Kong as lures, maintaining the dog's fascination with her chew toy. To further focus the dog's interest, I always make sure to flavor the triangular biscuits by rubbing them with a little cheese or freeze-dried liver.

If stuffed chew toys are reserved especially for times the dog is confined, the puppydog will soon learn to enjoy quiet moments in her doggy den and she will quickly develop a chew-toy habit— a good habit! This is a simple *autoshaping* process; all the owner has to do is set up the situation and the dog all but trains herself— easy and effective. Even when the dog is given run of the house, her first inclination will be to indulge her rewarding chew-toy habit rather than destroy less-attractive household articles, such as curtains, carpets, chairs and compact disks. Similarly, a chew-toy chewer will be less inclined to scratch and chew herself excessively. Also, if the dog busies herself as a recreational chewer, she will be less inclined to develop into a recreational barker or digger when left at home alone.

Stuff a number of chew toys whenever the dog is left confined and remove the extra-special-tasting treats when you return. Your dog will now amuse herself with her chew toys before falling asleep and then resume playing with her chew toys when she expects you to return. Since most owner-absent misbehavior happens right after you leave and right before your expected return, your puppydog will now be conveniently preoccupied with her chew toys at these times.

Come and Sit

Most puppies will happily approach virtually anyone, whether called or not; that is, until they collide with adolescence and

develop other more important doggy interests, such as sniffing a multiplicity of exquisite odors on the grass. Your mission, Mr./Ms. Owner, is to teach and reward the pup for coming reliably, willingly and happily when called—and you have just three months to get it done. Unless adequately reinforced, your puppy's tendency to approach people will self-destruct by adolescence.

Call your dog ("Tina, come!"), open your arms (and maybe squat down) as a welcoming signal, waggle a treat or toy as a lure and reward the puppydog when she comes running. Do not wait to praise the dog until she reaches you—she may come 95 percent of the way and then run off after some distraction. Instead, praise the dog's *first* step towards you and continue praising enthusiastically for *every* step she takes in your direction.

When the rapidly approaching puppy dog is three lengths away from impact, instruct her to sit ("Tina, sit!") and hold the lure in front of you in an outstretched hand to prevent her from hitting you mid-chest and knocking you flat on your back! As Tina decelerates to nose the lure, move the treat upwards and backwards just over her muzzle with an upwards motion of your extended arm (palm-upwards). As the dog looks up to follow the lure, she will sit down (if she jumps up, you are holding the lure too high). Praise the dog for sitting. Move backwards and call her again. Repeat this many times over, always praising when Tina comes and sits; on occasion, reward her.

For the first couple of trials, use a training treat both as a lure to entice the dog to come and sit and as a reward for doing so. Thereafter, try to use different items as lures and rewards. For example, lure the dog with a Kong or Frisbee but reward her with a food treat. Or lure the dog with a food treat but pat her and throw a tennis ball as a reward. After just a few repetitions, dispense with the lures and rewards; the dog will begin to respond willingly to your verbal requests and hand signals just for the prospect of praise from your heart and affection from your hands.

Instruct every family member, friend and visitor how to get the dog to come and sit. Invite people over for a series of pooch parties; do not keep the pup a secret—let other people enjoy this puppy, and let the pup enjoy other people. Puppydog parties are not only fun, they easily attract a lot of people to help *you* train *your* dog. Unless you teach your dog how to meet people, that is, to sit for greetings, no doubt the dog will resort to jumping up. Then you and the visitors will get annoyed, and the dog will be punished. This is not fair. *Send out those invitations for puppy parties and teach your dog to be mannerly and socially acceptable.*

Even though your dog quickly masters obedient recalls in the house, her reliability may falter when playing in the backyard or local park. Ironically, it is *the owner* who has unintentionally trained the dog *not* to respond in these instances. By allowing the dog to play and run around and otherwise have a good time, but then to call the dog to put her on leash to take her home, the dog quickly learns playing is fun but training is a drag. Thus, playing in the park becomes a severe distraction, which works against training. Bad news!

Instead, whether playing with the dog off leash or on leash, request her to come at frequent intervals—say, every minute or so. On most occasions, praise and pet the dog for a few seconds while she is sitting, then tell her to go play again. For especially fast recalls, offer a couple of training treats and take the time to praise and pet the dog enthusiastically before releasing her. The dog will learn that coming when called is not necessarily the end of the play session, and neither is it the end of the world; rather, it signals an enjoyable, quality time-out with the owner before resuming play once more. In fact, playing in the park now becomes a very effective life-reward, which works to facilitate training by reinforcing each obedient and timely recall. Good news!

Sit, Down, Stand and Rollover

Teaching the dog a variety of body positions is easy for owner and dog, impressive for spectators and extremely useful for all. Using lure-reward techniques, it is possible to train several positions at once to verbal commands or hand signals (which impress the socks off onlookers).

Sit and **down**—the two control commands—prevent or resolve nearly a hundred behavior problems. For example, if the dog happily and obediently sits or lies down when requested, she cannot jump on visitors, dash out the front door, run around and chase her tail, pester other dogs, harass cats or annoy family, friends or strangers. Additionally, "Sit" or "Down" are the best emergency commands for off-leash control.

It is easier to teach and maintain a reliable sit than maintain a reliable recall. *Sit* is the purest and simplest of commands—either the dog is sitting or she is not. If there is any change of circumstances or potential danger in the park, for example, simply instruct the dog to sit. If she sits, you have a number of options: Allow the dog to resume playing when she is safe, walk up and put the dog on leash or call the dog. The dog will be much more likely to come when called if she has already acknowledged her compliance by sitting. If the dog does not sit in the park—train her to!

Stand and **rollover-stay** are the two positions for examining the dog. Your veterinarian will love you to distraction if you take a little time to teach the dog to stand still and roll over and play possum. Also, your vet bills will be smaller because it will take the veterinarian less time to examine your dog. The rollover-stay is an especially useful command and is really just a variation of the down-stay: Whereas the dog lies prone in the traditional down, she lies supine in the rollover-stay.

As with teaching come and sit, the training techniques to teach the dog to assume all other body positions on cue are user-friendly and dog-friendly. Simply give the appropriate request, lure the dog into the desired body position using a training treat or toy and then *praise* (and maybe reward) the dog as soon as she complies. Try not to touch the dog to get her to respond. If you teach the dog by guiding her into position, the dog will quickly learn that rump-pressure means sit, for example, but as yet you still have no control over your dog if she is just 6 feet away. It will still be necessary to teach the dog to sit on request. So do not make training a time-consuming two-step process; instead, teach the dog to sit to a verbal request or hand signal from the outset. Once the dog sits willingly when requested, by all means use your hands to pet the dog when she does so.

To teach *down* when the dog is already sitting, say "Tina, down!," hold the lure in one hand (palm down) and lower that hand to the floor between the dog's forepaws. As the dog lowers her head to follow the lure, slowly move the lure away from the dog just a fraction (in front of her paws). The dog will lie down as she stretches her nose forward to follow the lure. Praise the dog when she does so. If the dog stands up, you pulled the lure away too far and too quickly.

When teaching the dog to lie down from the standing position, say "Down" and lower the lure to the floor as before. Once the dog has lowered her forequarters and assumed a play bow, gently and slowly move the lure *towards* the dog between her forelegs. Praise the dog as soon as her rear end plops down.

After just a couple of trials it will be possible to alternate sits and downs and have the dog energetically perform doggy push-ups. Praise the dog a lot, and after half a dozen or so push-ups reward the dog with a training treat or toy. You will notice the more energetically you move your arm—upwards (palm up) to get the dog to sit, and downwards (palm down) to get the dog to lie down—the more energetically the dog responds to your requests. Now try training the dog in silence and you will notice she has also learned to respond to hand signals. Yeah! Not too shabby for the first session.

To teach **stand** from the sitting position, say "Tina, stand," slowly move the lure half a dog-length away from the dog's nose, keeping it at nose level, and praise the dog as she stands to follow the lure. As soon

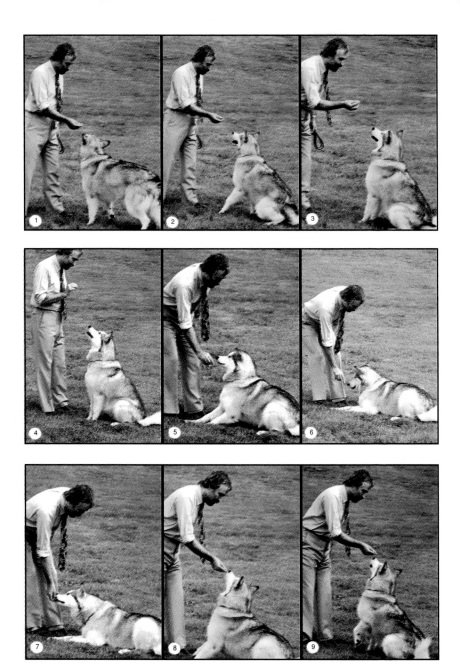

Using a food lure to teach sit, down and stand. 1) "Phoenix, sit." 2) Hand palm upwards, move lure up and back over dog's muzzle. 3) "Good sit, Phoenix!" 4) "Phoenix, down." 5) Hand palm downwards, move lure down to lie between dog's forepaws. 6) "Phoenix, off. Good down, Phoenix!" 7) "Phoenix, sit!" 8) Palm upwards, move lure up and back, keeping it close to dog's muzzle. 9) "Good sit, Phoenix!"

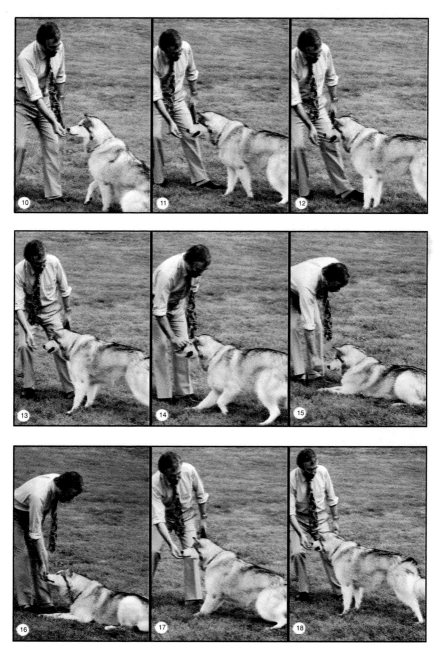

10) "Phoenix, stand!" 11) Move lure away from dog at nose height, then lower it a tad. 12) "Phoenix, off! Good stand, Phoenix!" 13) "Phoenix, down!" 14) Hand palm downwards, move lure down to lie between dog's forepaws. 15) "Phoenix, off! Good down-stay, Phoenix!" 16) "Phoenix, stand!" 17) Move lure away from dog's muzzle up to nose height. 18) "Phoenix, off! Good stand-stay, Phoenix. Now we'll make the vet and groomer happy!"

as the dog stands, lower the lure to just beneath the dog's chin to entice her to look down; otherwise she will stand and then sit immediately. To prompt the dog to stand from the down position, move the lure half a dog-length upwards and away from the dog, holding the lure at standing nose height from the floor.

Teaching *rollover* is best started from the down position, with the dog lying on one side, or at least with both hind legs stretched out on the same side. Say "Tina, bang!" and move the lure backwards and alongside the dog's muzzle to her elbow (on the side of her outstretched hind legs). Once the dog looks to the side and backwards, very slowly move the lure upwards to the dog's shoulder and backbone. Tickling the dog in the goolies (groin area) often invokes a reflex-raising of the hind leg as an appeasement gesture, which facilitates the tendency to roll over. If you move the lure too quickly and the dog jumps into the standing position, have patience and start again. As soon as the dog rolls onto her back, keep the lure stationary and mesmerize the dog with a relaxing tummy rub.

To teach *rollover-stay* when the dog is standing or moving, say "Tina, bang!" and give the appropriate hand signal (with index finger pointed and thumb cocked in true Sam Spade fashion), then in one fluid movement lure her to first lie down and then rollover-stay as above.

Teaching the dog to *stay* in each of the above four positions becomes a piece of cake after first teaching the dog not to worry at the toy or treat training lure. This is best accomplished by hand feeding dinner kibble. Hold a piece of kibble firmly in your hand and softly instruct "Off!" Ignore any licking and slobbering *for however long the dog worries at the treat*, but say "Take it!" and offer the kibble *the instant* the dog breaks contact with her muzzle. Repeat this a few times, and then up the ante and insist the dog remove her muzzle for one whole second before offering the kibble. Then progressively refine your criteria and have the dog not touch your hand (or treat) for longer and longer periods on each trial, such as for two seconds, four seconds, then six, ten, fifteen, twenty, thirty seconds and so on.

The dog soon learns: (1) worrying at the treat never gets results, whereas (2) noncontact is often rewarded after a variable time lapse.

Teaching *"Off!"* has many useful applications in its own right. Additionally, instructing the dog not to touch a training lure often produces spontaneous and magical stays. Request the dog to stand-stay, for example, and not to touch the lure. At first set your sights on a short two-second stay before rewarding the dog. (Remember, every long journey begins with a single step.) However, on subsequent trials, gradually and progressively increase the length of stay required to receive a reward. In no time at all your dog will stand calmly for a minute or so.

Relevancy Training

Once you have taught the dog what you expect her to do when requested to come, sit, lie down, stand, roll-over and stay, the time is right to teach the dog *why* she should comply with your wishes. The secret is to have many (*many*) extremely short training interludes (two to five seconds each) at numerous (*numerous*) times during the course of the dog's day. Especially work with the dog immediately *before* the dog's good times and *during* the dog's good times. For example, ask your dog to sit and/or lie down each time before opening doors, serving meals, offering treats and tummy rubs; ask the dog to perform a few controlled doggy push-ups before letting her off leash or throwing a tennis ball; and perhaps request the dog to sit-down-sit-stand-down-stand-rollover before inviting her to cuddle on the couch.

Similarly, request the dog to sit many times during play or on walks, and in no time at all the dog will be only too pleased to follow your instructions because she has learned that a compliant response heralds all sorts of goodies. Basically all you are trying to teach the dog is how to say please: "Please throw the tennis ball. Please may I snuggle on the couch."

Remember, it is important to keep training interludes short and to have many short sessions each and every day. The shortest (and most useful) session comprises asking the dog to sit and then go play during a play session. When trained this way, your dog will soon associate training with good times. In fact, the dog may be unable to distinguish between training and good times and, indeed, there should be no distinction. The warped concept that training involves forcing the dog to comply and/or dominating her will is totally at odds with the picture of a truly well-trained dog. In reality, enjoying a game of training with a dog is no different from enjoying a game of backgammon or tennis with a friend; and walking with a dog should be no different from strolling with a spouse, or with buddies on the golf course.

Walk by Your Side

Many people attempt to teach a dog to heel by putting her on a leash and physically correcting the dog when she makes mistakes. There are a number of things seriously wrong with this approach, the first being that most people do not want precision heeling; rather, they simply want the dog to follow or walk by their side. Second, when physically restrained during "training," even though the dog may grudgingly mope by your side when "handcuffed" on leash, let's see what happens when she is off leash. History! The dog is in the next county because she never enjoyed walking with you on leash and you have no control over her off leash. So let's just teach the dog off leash from the outset to *want* to walk with us. Third, if the dog has not been trained to heel, it is a trifle hasty to think about punishing the poor dog for making mistakes and breaking heeling rules she didn't even know existed. This is simply not fair! Surely, if the dog had been adequately taught how to heel, she would seldom make mistakes and hence there would be no need to correct the dog. Remember, each mistake and each correction (punishment) advertise the trainer's inadequacy, not the dog's. The dog is not stubborn, she is not stupid and she is not bad. Even if she were, she would still require training, so let's train her properly.

Let's teach the dog to *enjoy* following us and to *want* to walk by our side off leash. Then it will be easier to teach high-precision off-leash heeling patterns if desired. Before going on outdoor walks, it is necessary to teach the dog not to pull. Then it becomes easy to teach on-leash walking and heeling because the dog already wants to walk with you, she is familiar with the desired walking and heeling positions and she knows not to pull.

FOLLOWING

Start by training your dog to follow you. Many puppies will follow if you simply walk away from them and maybe click your fingers or chuckle. Adult dogs may require additional enticement to stimulate them to follow, such as a training lure or, at the very least, a lively trainer. To teach the dog to follow: (1) keep walking and (2) walk away from the dog. If the dog attempts to lead or lag, change pace; slow down if the dog forges too far ahead, but speed up if she lags too far behind. Say "Steady!" or "Easy!" each time before you slow down and "Quickly!" or "Hustle!" each time before you speed up, and the dog will learn to change pace on cue. If the dog lags or leads too far, or if she wanders right or left, simply walk quickly in the opposite direction and maybe even run away from the dog and hide.

Practicing is a lot of fun; you can set up a course in your home, yard or park to do this. Indoors, entice the dog to follow upstairs, into a bedroom, into the bathroom, downstairs, around the living room couch, zigzagging between dining room chairs and into the kitchen for dinner. Outdoors, get the dog to follow around park benches, trees, shrubs and along walkways and lines in the grass. (For safety outdoors, it is advisable to attach a long line on the dog, but never exert corrective tension on the line.)

Remember, following has a lot to do with attitude—*your* attitude! Most probably your dog will *not* want to follow Mr. Grumpy Troll with the personality of wilted lettuce. Lighten up—walk with a jaunty step, whistle a happy tune, sing, skip and tell jokes to your dog and she will be right there by your side.

BY YOUR SIDE

It is smart to train the dog to walk close on one side or the other—either side will do, your choice. When walking, jogging or cycling, it is generally bad news to have the dog suddenly cut in front of you. In fact, I train my dogs to walk "By my side" and "Other side"—both very useful instructions. It is possible to position the dog fairly accurately by looking to the appropriate side and clicking your fingers or slapping your thigh on that side. A precise positioning may be attained by holding a training lure, such as a chew toy, tennis ball or food treat. Stop and stand still several times throughout the walk, just as you would when window shopping or meeting a friend. Use the lure to make sure the dog slows down and stays close whenever you stop.

When teaching the dog to heel, we generally want her to sit in heel position when we stop. Teach heel

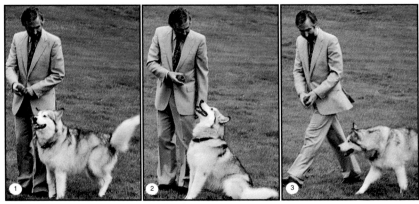

Using a toy to teach sit-heel-sit sequences: 1) "Phoenix, sit!" Standing still, move lure up and back over dog's muzzle . . . 2) to position dog sitting in heel position on your left side. 3) Say "Phoenix, heel!" and walk ahead, wagging lure in left hand. Change lure to right hand in preparation for sit signal. Say "Sit" and then . . .

122

position at the standstill and the dog will learn that the default heel position is sitting by your side (left or right—your choice, unless you wish to compete in obedience trials, in which case the dog must heel on the left).

Several times a day, stand up and call your dog to come and sit in heel position—"Tina, heel!" For example, instruct the dog to come to heel each time there are commercials on TV, or each time you turn a page of a novel, and the dog will get it in a single evening.

Practice straight-line heeling and turns separately. With the dog sitting at heel, teach her to turn in place. After each quarter-turn, half-turn or full turn in place, lure the dog to sit at heel. Now it's time for short straight-line heeling sequences, no more than a few steps at a time. Always think of heeling in terms of sit-heel-sit sequences—start and end with the dog in position and do your best to keep her there when moving. Progressively increase the number of steps in each sequence. When the dog remains close for 20 yards of straight-line heeling, it is time to add a few turns and then sign up for a happy-heeling obedience class to get some advice from the experts.

4) use hand signal to lure dog to sit as you stop. Eventually, dog will sit automatically at heel whenever you stop. 5) "Good dog!"

No Pulling on Leash

You can start teaching your dog not to pull on leash anywhere—in front of the television or outdoors—but regardless of location, you must not take a single step with tension in the leash. For a reason known only to dogs, even just a couple of paces of pulling on leash is intrinsically motivating and diabolically rewarding. Instead, attach the leash to the dog's collar, grasp the other end firmly with both hands held close to your chest, and stand still—do not budge an inch. Have somebody watch you with a stopwatch to time your progress, or else you will never believe this will work and so you will not even try the exercise, and your shoulder and the dog's neck will be traumatized for years to come.

Stand still and wait for the dog to stop pulling, and to sit and/or lie down. All dogs stop pulling and sit eventually. Most take only a couple of minutes; the all-time record is 22½ minutes. Time how long it takes. Gently praise the dog when she stops pulling, and as soon as she sits, enthusiastically praise the dog and take just one step forward, then immediately stand still. This single step usually demonstrates the ballistic reinforcing nature of pulling on leash; most dogs explode to the end of the leash, so be prepared for the strain. Stand firm and wait for the dog to sit again. Repeat this half a dozen times and you will probably notice a progressive reduction in the force of the dog's one-step explosions and a radical reduction in the time it takes for the dog to sit each time.

As the dog learns "Sit we go" and "Pull we stop," she will begin to walk forward calmly with each single step and automatically sit when you stop. Now try two steps before you stop. Wooooooo! Scary! When the dog has mastered two steps at a time, try for three. After each success, progressively increase the number of steps in the sequence: try four steps and then six, eight, ten and twenty steps before stopping. Congratulations! You are now walking the dog on leash.

Whenever walking with the dog (off leash or on leash), make sure you stop periodically to practice a few position commands and stays before instructing the dog to "Walk on!" (Remember, you want the dog to be compliant everywhere, not just in the kitchen when her dinner is at hand.) For example, stopping every 25 yards to briefly train the dog amounts to over 200 training interludes within a single 3-mile stroll. And each training session is in a different location. You will not believe the improvement within just the first mile of the first walk.

To put it another way, integrating training into a walk offers 200 separate opportunities to use the continuance of the walk as a reward to reinforce the dog's education. Moreover, some training interludes may comprise continuing education for the dog's walking skills: Alternate short periods of the dog walking calmly by your side with periods when the dog is allowed to sniff and investigate the environment. Now sniffing odors on the grass and meeting other dogs become rewards which reinforce the dog's calm and mannerly demeanor. Good Lord! Whatever next? Many enjoyable walks together of course. Happy trails!

THE IMPORTANCE OF TRICKS

Nothing will improve a dog's quality of life better than having a few tricks under her belt. Teaching any trick expands the dog's vocabulary, which facilitates communication and improves the owner's control. Also, specific tricks help prevent and resolve specific behavior problems. For example, by teaching the dog to fetch her toys, the dog learns carrying a toy makes the owner happy and, therefore, will be more likely to chew her toy than other inappropriate items.

More important, teaching tricks prompts owners to lighten up and train with a sunny disposition. Really, tricks should be no different from any other behaviors we put on cue. But they are. When teaching tricks, owners have a much sweeter attitude, which in turn motivates the dog and improves her willingness to comply. The dog feels tricks are a blast, but formal commands are a drag. In fact, tricks are so enjoyable, they may be used as rewards in training by asking the dog to come, sit and down-stay and then rollover for a tummy rub. Go on, try it: Crack a smile and even giggle when the dog promptly and willingly lies down and stays.

Most important, performing tricks prompts onlookers to smile and gig-gle. Many people are scared of dogs, especially large ones. And noth-ing can be more off-putting for a dog than to be constantly confronted by strangers who don't like her because of her size or the way she looks. Uneasy people put the dog on edge, causing her to back off and bark, only frightening people all the more. And so a vicious circle devel-ops, with the people's fear fueling the dog's fear *and vice versa*. Instead, tie a pink ribbon to your dog's collar and practice all sorts of tricks on walks and in the park, and you will be pleasantly amazed how it changes people's attitudes toward your friendly dog. The dog's reper-toire of tricks is limited only by the trainer's imagination. Below I have described three of my favorites:

SPEAK AND SHUSH

The training sequence involved in teaching a dog to bark on request is no different from that used when training any behavior on cue: request—lure—response—reward. As always, the secret of success lies in finding an effective lure. If the dog always barks at the doorbell, for example, say "Rover, speak!", have an accomplice ring the doorbell, then reward the dog for barking. After a few woofs, ask Rover to "Shush!", waggle a food treat under her nose (to entice her to sniff and thus to shush), praise her when quiet and eventually offer the treat as a reward. Alternate "Speak" and "Shush," progressively increasing the length of shush-time between each barking bout.

PLAY BOW

With the dog standing, say "Bow!" and lower the food lure (palm upwards) to rest between the dog's forepaws. Praise as the dog lowers her forequarters and sternum to the ground (as when teaching the down), but then lure the dog to stand and offer the treat. On successive trials, gradually increase the length of time the dog is required to remain in the play bow posture in order to gain a food reward. If the dog's rear end collapses into a down, say nothing and offer no reward; simply start over.

BE A BEAR

With the dog sitting backed into a corner to prevent her from toppling over backwards, say "Be a bear!" With bent paw and palm down, raise a lure upwards and backwards along the top of the dog's muzzle. Praise the dog when she sits up on her haunches and offer the treat as a reward. To prevent the dog from standing on her hind legs, keep the lure closer to the dog's muzzle. On each trial, progressively increase the length of time the dog is required to sit up to receive a food reward. Since lure-reward training is so easy, teach the dog to stand and walk on her hind legs as well!

Teaching "Be a Bear"

chapter 9

Getting
Active
with your Dog

by Bardi McLennan

Once you and your dog have graduated from basic obedience training and are beginning to work together as a team, you can take part in the growing world of dog activities. There are so many fun things to do with your dog! Just remember, people and dogs don't always learn at the same pace, so don't be upset if you (or your dog) need more than two basic training courses before your team becomes operational. Even smart dogs don't go straight to college from kindergarten!

Just as there are events geared to certain types of dogs, so there are ones that are more appealing to certain types of people. In some activities, you give the commands and your dog does the work (upland game hunting is one example), while in others, such as agility, you'll both get a workout. You may want to aim for prestigious titles to add to your dog's name, or you may want nothing more than the sheer enjoyment of being around other people and their dogs. Passive or active, participation has its own rewards.

Consider your dog's physical capabilities when looking into any of the canine activities. It's easy to see that a Basset Hound is not built for the racetrack, nor would a Chihuahua be the breed of choice for pulling a sled. A loyal dog will attempt almost anything you ask him to do, so it is up to you to know your dog's limitations. A dog must be physically sound in order to compete at any level in athletic activities, and being mentally sound is a definite plus. Advanced age, however, may not be a deterrent. Many dogs still hunt and herd at ten or twelve years of age. It's entirely possible for dogs to be "fit at 50." Take your dog for a checkup, explain to your vet the type of activity you have in mind and be guided by his or her findings.

*All dogs seem
to love playing
flyball.*

You needn't be restricted to breed-specific sports if it's only fun you're after. Certain AKC activities are limited to designated breeds; however, as each new trial, test or sport has grown in popularity, so has the variety of breeds encouraged to participate at a fun level.

But don't shortchange your fun, or that of your dog, by thinking only of the basic function of her breed. Once a dog has learned how to learn, she can be taught to do just about anything as long as the size of the dog is right for the job and you both think it is fun and rewarding. In other words, you are a team.

To get involved in any of the activities detailed in this chapter, look for the names and addresses of the organizations that sponsor them in Chapter 13. You can also ask your breeder or a local dog trainer for contacts.

You can compete in obedience trials with a well trained dog.

Official American Kennel Club Activities

The following tests and trials are some of the events sanctioned by the AKC and sponsored by various dog clubs. Your dog's expertise will be rewarded with impressive titles. You can participate just for fun, or be competitive and go for those awards.

OBEDIENCE

Training classes begin with pups as young as three months of age in kindergarten puppy training, then advance to pre-novice (all exercises on lead) and go on to novice, which is where you'll start off-lead work. In obedience classes dogs learn to sit, stay, heel and come through a variety of exercises. Once you've got the basics down, you can enter obedience trials and work toward earning your dog's first degree, a C.D. (Companion Dog).

The next level is called "Open," in which jumps and retrieves perk up the dog's interest. Passing grades in competition at this level earn a C.D.X. (Companion Dog Excellent). Beyond that lies the goal of the most ambitious—Utility (U.D. and even U.D.X. or OTCh, an Obedience Champion).

AGILITY

All dogs can participate in the latest canine sport to have gained worldwide popularity for its fun and excitement, agility. It began in England as a canine version of horse show-jumping, but because dogs are more agile and able to perform on verbal commands, extra feats were added such as climbing, balancing and racing through tunnels or in and out of weave poles. Many of the obstacles (regulation or homemade) can be set up in your own backyard. If the agility bug bites, you could end up in international competition!

For starters, your dog should be obedience trained, even though, in the beginning, the lessons may all be taught on lead. Once the dog understands the commands (and you do, too), it's as easy as guiding the dog over a prescribed course, one obstacle at a time. In competition, the race is against the clock, so wear your running shoes! The dog starts with 200 points and the judge deducts for infractions and misadventures along the way.

All dogs seem to love agility and respond to it as if they were being turned loose in a playground paradise. Your dog's enthusiasm will be contagious; agility turns into great fun for dog and owner.

FIELD TRIALS AND HUNTING TESTS

There are field trials and hunting tests for the sporting breeds—retrievers, spaniels and pointing breeds, and for some hounds—Bassets, Beagles and Dachshunds. Field trials are competitive events that test a dog's ability to perform the functions for which she was bred. Hunting tests, which are open to retrievers,

---

TITLES AWARDED BY THE AKC

Conformation: Ch. (Champion)

Obedience: CD (Companion Dog); CDX (Companion Dog Excellent); UD (Utility Dog); UDX (Utility Dog Excellent); OTCh. (Obedience Trial Champion)

Field: JH (Junior Hunter); SH (Senior Hunter); MH (Master Hunter); AFCh. (Amateur Field Champion); FCh. (Field Champion)

Lure Coursing: JC (Junior Courser); SC (Senior Courser)

Herding: HT (Herding Tested); PT (Pre-Trial Tested); HS (Herding Started); HI (Herding Intermediate); HX (Herding Excellent); HCh. (Herding Champion)

Tracking: TD (Tracking Dog); TDX (Tracking Dog Excellent)

Agility: NAD (Novice Agility); OAD (Open Agility); ADX (Agility Excellent); MAX (Master Agility)

Earthdog Tests: JE (Junior Earthdog); SE (Senior Earthdog); ME (Master Earthdog)

Canine Good Citizen: CGC

Combination: DC (Dual Champion—Ch. and Fch.); TC (Triple Champion—Ch., Fch., and OTCh.)

---

spaniels and pointing breeds only, are noncompetitive and are a means of judging the dog's ability as well as that of the handler.

Hunting is a very large and complex part of canine sports, and if you own one of the breeds that hunts, the events are a great treat for your dog and you. He gets to do what he was bred for, and you get to work with him and watch him do it. You'll be proud of and amazed at what your dog can do.

Fortunately, the AKC publishes a series of booklets on these events, which outline the rules and regulations and include a glossary of the sometimes complicated terms. The AKC also publishes newsletters for field trialers and hunting test enthusiasts. The United Kennel Club (UKC) also has informative materials for the hunter and his dog.

Retrievers and other sporting breeds get to do what they're bred to in hunting tests.

HERDING TESTS AND TRIALS

Herding, like hunting, dates back to the first known uses man made of dogs. The interest in herding today is widespread, and if you own a herding breed, you can join in the activity. Herding dogs are tested for their natural skills to keep a flock of ducks, sheep or cattle together. If your dog shows potential, you can start at the testing level, where your dog can earn a title for showing an inherent herding ability. With training you can advance to the trial level, where your dog should be capable of controlling even difficult livestock in diverse situations.

LURE COURSING

The AKC Tests and Trials for Lure Coursing are open to traditional sighthounds—Greyhounds, Whippets,

Borzoi, Salukis, Afghan Hounds, Ibizan Hounds and Scottish Deerhounds—as well as to Basenjis and Rhodesian Ridgebacks. Hounds are judged on overall ability, follow, speed, agility and endurance. This is possibly the most exciting of the trials for spectators, because the speed and agility of the dogs is awesome to watch as they chase the lure (or "course") in heats of two or three dogs at a time.

TRACKING

Tracking is another activity in which almost any dog can compete because every dog that sniffs the ground when taken outdoors is, in fact, tracking. The hard part comes when the rules as to what, when and where the dog tracks are determined by a person, not the dog! Tracking tests cover a large area of fields, woods and roads. The tracks are laid hours before the dogs go to work on them, and include "tricks" like cross-tracks and sharp turns. If you're interested in search-and-rescue work, this is the place to start.

This tracking dog is hot on the trail.

EARTHDOG TESTS FOR SMALL TERRIERS AND DACHSHUNDS

These tests are open to Australian, Bedlington, Border, Cairn, Dandie Dinmont, Smooth and Wire Fox, Lakeland, Norfolk, Norwich, Scottish, Sealyham, Skye, Welsh and West Highland White Terriers as well as Dachshunds. The dogs need no prior training for this terrier sport. There is a qualifying test on the day of the event, so dog and handler learn the rules on the spot. These tests, or "digs," sometimes end with informal races in the late afternoon.

133

Here are some of the extracurricular obedience and racing activities that are not regulated by the AKC or UKC, but are generally run by clubs or a group of dog fanciers and are often open to all.

Canine Freestyle This activity is something new on the scene and is variously likened to dancing, dressage or ice skating. It is meant to show the athleticism of the dog, but also requires showmanship on the part of the dog's handler. If you and your dog like to ham it up for friends, you might want to look into freestyle.

Lure coursing lets sighthounds do what they do best—run!

Scent Hurdle Racing Scent hurdle racing is purely a fun activity sponsored by obedience clubs with members forming competing teams. The height of the hurdles is based on the size of the shortest dog on the team. On a signal, one team dog is released on each of two side-by-side courses and must clear every hurdle before picking up its own dumbbell from a platform and returning over the jumps to the handler. As each dog returns, the next on that team is sent. Of course, that is what the dogs are supposed to do. When the dogs improvise (going under or around the hurdles, stealing another dog's dumbbell, and so forth), it no doubt frustrates the handlers, but just adds to the fun for everyone else.

Flyball This type of racing is similar, but after negotiating the four hurdles, the dog comes to a flyball box, steps on a lever that releases a tennis ball into the air, catches the ball and returns over the hurdles to the starting point. This game also becomes extremely fun for spectators because the dogs sometimes cheat by catching a ball released by the dog in the next lane. Three titles can be earned—Flyball Dog (F.D.), Flyball Dog Excellent (F.D.X.) and Flyball Dog Champion (Fb.D.Ch.)—all awarded by the North American Flyball Association, Inc.

Dogsledding The name conjures up the Rocky Mountains or the frigid North, but you can find dogsled clubs in such unlikely spots as Maryland, North Carolina and Virginia! Dogsledding is primarily for the Nordic breeds such as the Alaskan Malamutes, Siberian Huskies and Samoyeds, but other breeds can try. There are some practical backyard applications to this sport, too. With parental supervision, almost any strong dog could pull a child's sled.

Coming over the A-frame on an agility course.

These are just some of the many recreational ways you can get to know and understand your multifaceted dog better and have fun doing it.

Your Dog
and your
Family

by Bardi McLennan

Adding a dog automatically increases your family by one, no matter whether you live alone in an apartment or are part of a mother, father and six kids household. The single-person family is fair game for numerous and varied canine misconceptions as to who is dog and who pays the bills, whereas a dog in a houseful of children will consider himself to be just one of the gang, littermates all. One dog and one child may give a dog reason to believe they are both kids or both dogs. Either interpretation requires parental supervision and sometimes speedy intervention.

As soon as one paw goes through the door into your home, Rufus (or Rufina) has to make many adjustments to become a part of your family. Your job is to make him fit in as painlessly as possible. An older dog may have some frame of reference from past experience, but to a 10-week-old puppy, everything is brand new: people, furniture, stairs, when and where people eat, sleep or watch TV, his own place and everyone else's space, smells, sounds, outdoors—everything!

Puppies, and newly acquired dogs of any age, do not need what we think of as "freedom." If you leave a new dog or puppy loose in the house, you will almost certainly return to chaotic destruction and the dog will forever after equate your homecoming with a time of punishment to be dreaded. It is unfair to give your dog what amounts to "freedom to get into trouble." Instead, confine him to a crate for brief periods of your absence (up to three or four hours) and, for the long haul, a workday for example, confine him to one untrashable area with his own toys, a bowl of water and a radio left on (low) in another room.

Lots of pets get along with each other just fine.

For the first few days, when not confined, put Rufus on a long leash tied to your wrist or waist. This umbilical cord method enables the dog to learn all about you from your body language and voice, and to learn by his own actions which things in the house are NO! and which ones are rewarded by "Good dog." House-training will be easier with the pup always by your side. Speaking of which, accidents do happen. That goal of "completely housetrained" takes up to a year, or the length of time it takes the pup to mature.

The All-Adult Family

Most dogs in an adults-only household today are likely to be latchkey pets, with no one home all day but the dog. When you return after a tough day on the job, the dog can and should be your relaxation therapy. But going home can instead be a daily frustration.

Separation anxiety is a very common problem for the dog in a working household. It may begin with whines and barks of loneliness, but it will soon escalate into a frenzied destruction derby. That is why it is so important to set aside the time to teach a dog to relax when left alone in his confined area and to understand that he can trust you to return.

Let the dog get used to your work schedule in easy stages. Confine him to one room and go in and out of that room over and over again. Be casual about it. No physical, voice or eye contact. When the pup no longer even notices your comings and goings, leave the house for varying lengths of time, returning to stay home for a few minutes and gradually increasing the time away. This training can take days, but the dog is learning that you haven't left him forever and that he can trust you.

Any time you leave the dog, but especially during this training period, be casual about your departure. No anxiety-building fond farewells. Just "Bye" and go! Remember the "Good dog" when you return to find everything more or less as you left it.

If things are a mess (or even a disaster) when you return, greet the dog, take him outside to eliminate, and then put him in his crate while you clean up. Rant and rave in the shower! *Do not* punish the dog. You were not there when it happened, and the rule is: Only punish as you catch the dog in the act of wrongdoing. Obviously, it makes sense to get your latchkey puppy when you'll have a week or two to spend on these training essentials.

Family weekend activities should include Rufus whenever possible. Depending on the pup's age, now is the time for a long walk in the park, playtime in the backyard, a hike in the woods. Socializing is as important as health care, good food and physical exercise, so visiting Aunt Emma or Uncle Harry and the next-door neighbor's dog or cat is essential to developing an out-going, friendly temperament in your pet.

If you are a single adult, socializing Rufus at home and away will prevent him from becoming overly protective of you (or just overly attached) and will also prevent such behavioral problems as dominance or fear of strangers.

Babies

Whether already here or on the way, babies figure larger than life in the eyes of a dog. If the dog is there first, let him in on all your baby preparations in the house. When baby arrives, let Rufus sniff any item of clothing that has been on the baby before Junior comes home. Then let Mom greet the dog first before introducing the new family member. Hold the baby down for the dog to see and sniff, but make sure some-one's holding the dog on lead in case of any sudden moves. Don't play keep-away or tease the dog with the baby, which only invites undesirable jumping up.

The dog and the baby are "family," and for starters can be treated almost as equals. Things rapidly change, however, especially when baby takes to creeping around on all fours on the dog's turf or, better yet, has yummy pudding all over her face and hands! That's when a lot of things in the dog's and baby's lives become more separate than equal.

Dogs are perfect confidants.

Toddlers make terrible dog owners, but if you can't avoid the combination, use patient discipline (that is, positive teaching rather than punishment), and use time-outs before you run out of patience.

A dog and a baby (or toddler, or an assertive young child) should never be left alone together. Take the dog with you or confine him. With a baby or youngsters in the house, you'll have plenty of use for that wonderful canine safety device called a crate!

Young Children

Any dog in a house with kids will behave pretty much as the kids do, good or bad. But even good dogs and good children can get into trouble when play becomes rowdy and active.

Teach children how to play nicely with a puppy.

Legs bobbing up and down, shrill voices screeching, a ball hurtling overhead, all add up to exuberant frustration for a dog who's just trying to be part of the gang. In a pack of puppies, any legs or toys being chased would be caught by a set of teeth, and all the pups involved would understand that is how the game is played. Kids do not understand this, nor do parents tolerate it. Bring Rufus indoors before you have reason to regret it. This is time-out, not a punishment.

You can explain the situation to the children and tell them they must play quieter games until the puppy learns not to grab them with his mouth. Unfortunately, you can't explain it that easily to the dog. With adult supervision, they will learn how to play together.

Young children love to tease. Sticking their faces or wiggling their hands or fingers in the dog's face is teasing. To another person it might be just annoying, but it is threatening to a dog. There's another difference: We can make the child stop by an explanation, but the only way a dog can stop it is with a warning growl and then with teeth. Teasing is the major cause of children being bitten by their pets. Treat it seriously.

Older Children

The best age for a child to get a first dog is between the ages of 8 and 12. That's when kids are able to accept some real responsibility for their pet. Even so, take the child's vow of "I will never *ever* forget to feed (brush, walk, etc.) the dog" for what it's worth: a child's good intention at that moment. Most kids today have extra lessons, soccer practice, Little League, ballet, and so forth piled on top of school schedules. There will be many times when Mom will have to come to the dog's rescue. "I walked the dog for you so you can set the table for me" is one way to get around a missed appointment without laying on blame or guilt.

Kids in this age group make excellent obedience trainers because they are into the teaching/learning process themselves and they lack the self-consciousness of adults. Attending a dog show is something the whole family can enjoy, and watching Junior Showmanship may catch the eye of the kids. Older children can begin to get involved in many of the recreational activities that were reviewed in the previous chapter. Some of the agility obstacles, for example, can be set up in the backyard as a family project (with an adult making sure all the equipment is safe and secure for the dog).

Older kids are also beginning to look to the future, and may envision themselves as veterinarians or trainers or show dog handlers or writers of the next Lassie best-seller. Dogs are perfect confidants for these dreams. They won't tell a soul.

Other Pets

Introduce all pets tactfully. In a dog/cat situation, hold the dog, not the cat. Let two dogs meet on neutral turf—a stroll in the park or a walk down the street—with both on loose leads to permit all the normal canine ways of saying hello, including routine sniffing, circling, more sniffing, and so on. Small creatures such as hamsters, chinchillas or mice must be kept safe from their natural predators (dogs and cats).

Festive Family Occasions

Parties are great for people, but not necessarily for puppies. Until all the guests have arrived, put the dog in his crate or in a room where he won't be disturbed. A socialized dog can join the fun later as long as he's not underfoot, annoying guests or into the hors d'oeuvres.

There are a few dangers to consider, too. Doors opening and closing can allow a puppy to slip out unnoticed in the confusion, and you'll be organizing a search party instead of playing host or hostess. Party food and buffet service are not for dogs. Let Rufus party in his crate with a nice big dog biscuit.

At Christmas time, not only are tree decorations dangerous and breakable (and perhaps family heirlooms), but extreme caution should be taken with the lights, cords and outlets for the tree lights and any other festive lighting. Occasionally a dog lifts a leg, ignoring the fact that the tree is indoors. To avoid this, use a canine repellent, made for gardens, on the tree. Or keep him out of the tree room unless supervised. And whatever you do, *don't* invite trouble by hanging his toys on the tree!

Car Travel

Before you plan a vacation by car or RV with Rufus, be sure he enjoys car travel. Nothing spoils a holiday quicker than a carsick dog! Work within the dog's comfort level. Get in the car with the dog in his crate or attached to a canine car safety belt and just sit there until he relaxes. That's all. Next time, get in the car, turn on the engine and go nowhere. Just sit. When that is okay, turn on the engine and go around the block. Now you can go for a ride and include a stop where you get out, leaving the dog for a minute or two.

On a warm day, always park in the shade and leave windows open several inches. And return quickly. It only takes 10 minutes for a car to become an overheated steel death trap.

Motel or Pet Motel?

Not all motels or hotels accept pets, but you have a much better choice today than even a few years ago. To find a dog-friendly lodging, look at *On the Road Again With Man's Best Friend*, a series of directories that detail bed and breakfasts, inns, family resorts and other hotels/motels. Some places require a refundable deposit to cover any damage incurred by the dog. More B&Bs accept pets now, but some restrict the size.

If taking Rufus with you is not feasible, check out boarding kennels in your area. Your veterinarian may offer this service, or recommend a kennel or two he or she is familiar with. Go see the facilities for yourself, ask about exercise, diet, housing, and so on. Or, if you'd rather have Rufus stay home, look into bonded petsitters, many of whom will also bring in the mail and water your plants.

chapter 11

Your Dog

and your

Community

by Bardi McLennan

Step outside your home with your dog and you are no longer just family, you are both part of your community. This is when the phrase "responsible pet ownership" takes on serious implications. For starters, it means you pick up after your dog—not just occasionally, but every time your dog eliminates away from home. That means you have joined the Plastic Baggy Brigade! You always have plastic sandwich bags in your pocket and several in the car. It means you teach your kids how to use them, too. If you think this is "yucky," just imagine what

the person (a non-doggy person) who inadvertently steps in the mess thinks!

Your responsibility extends to your neighbors: To their ears (no annoying barking); to their property (their garbage, their lawn, their flower beds, their cat—especially their cat); to their kids (on bikes, at play); to their kids' toys and sports equipment.

There are numerous dog-related laws, ranging from simple dog licensing and leash laws to those holding you liable for any physical injury or property damage done by your dog. These laws are in place to protect everyone in the community, including you and your dog. There are town ordinances and state laws which are by no means the same in all towns or all states. Ignorance of the law won't get you off the hook. The time to find out what the laws are where you live is now.

Be sure your dog's license is current. This is not just a good local ordinance, it can make the difference between finding your lost dog or not.

Dressing your dog up makes him appealing to strangers.

Many states now require proof of rabies vaccination and that the dog has been spayed or neutered before issuing a license. At the same time, keep up the dog's annual immunizations.

Never let your dog run loose in the neighborhood. This will not only keep you, on the right side of the leash law, it's the outdoor version of the rule about not giving your dog "freedom to get into trouble."

Good Canine Citizen

Sometimes it's hard for a dog's owner to assess whether or not the dog is sufficiently socialized to be accepted by the community at large. Does Rufus or Rufina display good, controlled behavior in public? The AKC's Canine Good Citizen program is available through many dog organizations. If your dog passes the test, the title "CGC" is earned.

The overall purpose is to turn your dog into a good neighbor and to teach you about your responsibility to your community as a dog owner. Here are the ten things your dog must do willingly:

1. Accept a stranger stopping to chat with you.
2. Sit and be petted by a stranger.
3. Allow a stranger to handle him or her as a groomer or veterinarian would.
4. Walk nicely on a loose lead.
5. Walk calmly through a crowd.
6. Sit and down on command, then stay in a sit or down position while you walk away.
7. Come when called.
8. Casually greet another dog.
9. React confidently to distractions.
10. Accept being left alone with someone other than you and not become overly agitated or nervous.

Schools and Dogs

Schools are getting involved with pet ownership on an educational level. It has been proven that children who are kind to animals are humane in their attitude toward other people as adults.

A dog is a child's best friend, and so children are often primary pet owners, if not the primary caregivers. Unfortunately, they are also the ones most often bitten by dogs. This occurs due to a lack of understanding that pets, no matter how sweet, cuddly and loving, are still animals. Schools, along with parents, dog clubs, dog fanciers and the AKC, are working to change all that with video programs for children not only in grade school, but in the nursery school and pre-kindergarten age group. Teaching youngsters how to be responsible dog owners is important community work. When your dog has a CGC, volunteer to take part in an educational classroom event put on by your dog club.

Boy Scout Merit Badge

A Merit Badge for Dog Care can be earned by any Boy Scout ages 11 to 18. The requirements are not easy, but amount to a complete course in responsible dog care and general ownership. Here are just a few of the things a Scout must do to earn that badge:

Point out ten parts of the dog using the correct names.

Give a report (signed by parent or guardian) on your care of the dog (feeding, food used, housing, exercising, grooming and bathing), plus what has been done to keep the dog healthy.

Explain the right way to obedience train a dog, and demonstrate three comments.

Several of the requirements have to do with health care, including first aid, handling a hurt dog, and the dangers of home treatment for a serious ailment.

The final requirement is to know the local laws and ordinances involving dogs.

There are similar programs for Girl Scouts and 4-H members.

Local Clubs

Local dog clubs are no longer in existence just to put on a yearly dog show. Today, they are apt to be the hub of the community's involvement with pets. Dog clubs conduct educational forums with big-name speakers, stage demonstrations of canine talent in a busy mall and take dogs of various breeds to schools for class-room discussion.

The quickest way to feel accepted as a member in a club is to volunteer your services! Offer to help with something—anything—and watch your popularity (and your interest) grow.

Therapy Dogs

Once your dog has earned that essential CGC and reliably demonstrates a steady, calm temperament, you could look into what therapy dogs are doing in your area.

Therapy dogs go with their owners to visit patients at hospitals or nursing homes, generally remaining on leash but able to coax a pat from a stiffened hand, a smile from a blank face, a few words from sealed lips or a hug from someone in need of love.

Nursing homes cover a wide range of patient care. Some specialize in care of the elderly, some in the treatment of specific illnesses, some in physical therapy. Children's facilities also welcome visits from trained therapy dogs for boosting morale in their pediatric patients. Hospice care for the terminally ill and the at-home care of AIDS patients are other areas where this canine visiting is desperately needed. Therapy dog training comes first.

Your dog can make a difference in lots of lives.

There is a lot more involved than just taking your nice friendly pooch to someone's bedside. Doing therapy dog work involves your own emotional stability as well as that of your dog. But once you have met all the requirements for this work, making the rounds once a week or once a month with your therapy dog is possibly the most rewarding of all community activities.

Disaster Aid

This community service is definitely not for everyone, partly because it is time-consuming. The initial training is rigorous, and there can be no let-up in the continuing workouts, because members are on call 24 hours a day to go wherever they are needed at a moment's notice. But if you think you would like to be able to assist in a disaster, look into search-and-rescue work. The network of search-and-rescue volunteers is worldwide, and all members of the American Rescue Dog Association (ARDA) who are qualified to do this work are volunteers who train and maintain their own dogs.

Physical Aid

Most people are familiar with Seeing Eye dogs, which serve as blind people's eyes, but not with all the other work that dogs are trained to do to assist the disabled. Dogs are also specially trained to pull wheelchairs, carry school books, pick up dropped objects, open and close doors. Some also are ears for the deaf. All these assistance-trained dogs, by the way, are allowed anywhere "No Pet" signs exist (as are therapy dogs when

properly identified). Getting started in any of this fascinating work requires a background in dog training and canine behavior, but there are also volunteer jobs ranging from answering the phone to cleaning out kennels to providing a foster home for a puppy. You have only to ask.

Making the rounds with your therapy dog can be very rewarding.

part four

Beyond the
Basics

chapter 12

Recommended Reading

Books

ABOUT HEALTH CARE

Ackerman, Lowell. *Guide to Skin and Haircoat Problems in Dogs.* Loveland, Colo.: Alpine Publications, 1994.

Alderton, David. *The Dog Care Manual.* Hauppauge, N.Y.: Barron's Educational Series, Inc., 1986.

American Kennel Club. *American Kennel Club Dog Care and Training.* New York: Howell Book House, 1991.

Bamberger, Michelle, DVM. *Help! The Quick Guide to First Aid for Your Dog.* New York: Howell Book House, 1995.

Carlson, Delbert, DVM, and James Giffin, MD. *Dog Owner's Home Veterinary Handbook.* New York: Howell Book House, 1992.

DeBitetto, James, DVM, and Sarah Hodgson. *You & Your Puppy.* New York: Howell Book House, 1995.

Humphries, Jim, DVM. *Dr. Jim's Animal Clinic for Dogs.* New York: Howell Book House, 1994.

McGinnis, Terri. *The Well Dog Book.* New York: Random House, 1991.

Pitcairn, Richard and Susan. *Natural Health for Dogs.* Emmaus, Pa.: Rodale Press, 1982.

ABOUT DOG SHOWS

Hall, Lynn. *Dog Showing for Beginners.* New York: Howell Book House, 1994.

Nichols, Virginia Tuck. *How to Show Your Own Dog.* Neptune, N. J.: TFH, 1970.

Vanacore, Connie. *Dog Showing, An Owner's Guide.* New York: Howell Book House, 1990.

ABOUT TRAINING

Ammen, Amy. *Training in No Time*. New York: Howell Book House, 1995.

Baer, Ted. *Communicating With Your Dog*. Hauppauge, N.Y.: Barron's Educational Series, Inc., 1989.

Benjamin, Carol Lea. *Dog Problems*. New York: Howell Book House, 1989.

Benjamin, Carol Lea. *Dog Training for Kids*. New York: Howell Book House, 1988.

Benjamin, Carol Lea. *Mother Knows Best*. New York: Howell Book House, 1985.

Benjamin, Carol Lea. *Surviving Your Dog's Adolescence*. New York: Howell Book House, 1993.

Bohnenkamp, Gwen. *Manners for the Modern Dog*. San Francisco: Perfect Paws, 1990.

Dibra, Bashkim. *Dog Training by Bash*. New York: Dell, 1992.

Dunbar, Ian, PhD, MRCVS. *Dr. Dunbar's Good Little Dog Book*, James & Kenneth Publishers, 2140 Shattuck Ave. #2406, Berkeley, Calif. 94704. (510) 658–8588. Order from the publisher.

Dunbar, Ian, PhD, MRCVS. *How to Teach a New Dog Old Tricks*, James & Kenneth Publishers. Order from the publisher; address above.

Dunbar, Ian, PhD, MRCVS, and Gwen Bohnenkamp. Booklets on *Preventing Aggression; Housetraining; Chewing; Digging; Barking; Socialization; Fearfulness; and Fighting*, James & Kenneth Publishers. Order from the publisher; address above.

Evans, Job Michael. *People, Pooches and Problems*. New York: Howell Book House, 1991.

Kilcommons, Brian and Sarah Wilson. *Good Owners, Great Dogs*. New York: Warner Books, 1992.

McMains, Joel M. *Dog Logic—Companion Obedience*. New York: Howell Book House, 1992.

Rutherford, Clarice and David H. Neil, MRCVS. *How to Raise a Puppy You Can Live With*. Loveland, Colo.: Alpine Publications, 1982.

Volhard, Jack and Melissa Bartlett. *What All Good Dogs Should Know: The Sensible Way to Train*. New York: Howell Book House, 1991.

ABOUT BREEDING

Harris, Beth J. Finder. *Breeding a Litter, The Complete Book of Prenatal and Postnatal Care*. New York: Howell Book House, 1983.

Holst, Phyllis, DVM. *Canine Reproduction*. Loveland, Colo.: Alpine Publications, 1985.

Walkowicz, Chris and Bonnie Wilcox, DVM. *Successful Dog Breeding, The Complete Handbook of Canine Midwifery*. New York: Howell Book House, 1994.

ABOUT ACTIVITIES

American Rescue Dog Association. *Search and Rescue Dogs*. New York: Howell Book House, 1991.

Barwig, Susan and Stewart Hilliard. *Schutzhund*. New York: Howell Book House, 1991.

Beaman, Arthur S. *Lure Coursing*. New York: Howell Book House, 1994.

Daniels, Julie. *Enjoying Dog Agility—From Backyard to Competition*. New York: Doral Publishing, 1990.

Davis, Kathy Diamond. *Therapy Dogs*. New York: Howell Book House, 1992.

Gallup, Davis Anne. *Running With Man's Best Friend*. Loveland, Colo.: Alpine Publications, 1986.

Habgood, Dawn and Robert. *On the Road Again With Man's Best Friend*. New England, Mid-Atlantic, West Coast and Southeast editions. Selective guides to area bed and breakfasts, inns, hotels and resorts that welcome guests and their dogs. New York: Howell Book House, 1995.

Holland, Vergil S. *Herding Dogs*. New York: Howell Book House, 1994.

LaBelle, Charlene G. *Backpacking With Your Dog*. Loveland, Colo.: Alpine Publications, 1993.

Simmons-Moake, Jane. *Agility Training, The Fun Sport for All Dogs*. New York: Howell Book House, 1991.

Spencer, James B. *Hup! Training Flushing Spaniels the American Way*. New York: Howell Book House, 1992.

Spencer, James B. *Point! Training the All-Seasons Birddog*. New York: Howell Book House, 1995.

Tarrant, Bill. *Training the Hunting Retriever*. New York: Howell Book House, 1991.

Volhard, Jack and Wendy. *The Canine Good Citizen*. New York: Howell Book House, 1994.

General Titles

Haggerty, Captain Arthur J. *How to Get Your Pet Into Show Business*. New York: Howell Book House, 1994.

McLennan, Bardi. *Dogs and Kids, Parenting Tips*. New York: Howell Book House, 1993.

Moran, Patti J. *Pet Sitting for Profit, A Complete Manual for Professional Success*. New York: Howell Book House, 1992.

Scalisi, Danny and Libby Moses. *When Rover Just Won't Do, Over 2,000 Suggestions for Naming Your Dog.* New York: Howell Book House, 1993.

Sife, Wallace, PhD. *The Loss of a Pet.* New York: Howell Book House, 1993.

Wrede, Barbara J. *Civilizing Your Puppy.* Hauppauge, N.Y.: Barron's Educational Series, 1992.

Magazines

The AKC GAZETTE, The Official Journal for the Sport of Purebred Dogs. American Kennel Club, 51 Madison Ave., New York, NY.

Bloodlines Journal. United Kennel Club, 100 E. Kilgore Rd., Kalamazoo, MI.

Dog Fancy. Fancy Publications, 3 Burroughs, Irvine, CA 92718

Dog World. Maclean Hunter Publishing Corp., 29 N. Wacker Dr., Chicago, IL 60606.

Videos

"SIRIUS Puppy Training," by Ian Dunbar, PhD, MRCVS. James & Kenneth Publishers, 2140 Shattuck Ave. #2406, Berkeley, CA 94704. Order from the publisher.

"Training the Companion Dog," from Dr. Dunbar's British TV Series, James & Kenneth Publishers. (See address above).

The American Kennel Club produces videos on every breed of dog, as well as on hunting tests, field trials and other areas of interest to purebred dog owners. For more information, write to AKC/Video Fulfillment, 5580 Centerview Dr., Suite 200, Raleigh, NC 27606.

13

Resources

Breed Clubs

Every breed recognized by the American Kennel Club has a national (parent) club. National clubs are a great source of information on your breed. You can get the name of the secretary of the club by contacting:

The American Kennel Club
51 Madison Avenue
New York, NY 10010
(212) 696-8200

There are also numerous all-breed, individual breed, obedience, hunting and other special-interest dog clubs across the country. The American Kennel Club can provide you with a geographical list of clubs to find ones in your area. Contact them at the above address.

Registry Organizations

Registry organizations register purebred dogs. The American Kennel Club is the oldest and largest in this country, and currently recognizes over 130 breeds. The United Kennel Club registers some breeds the AKC doesn't (including the American Pit Bull Terrier and the Miniature Fox Terrier) as well as many of the same breeds. The others included here are for your reference; the AKC can provide you with a list of foreign registries.

American Kennel Club
51 Madison Avenue
New York, NY 10010

United Kennel Club (UKC)
100 E. Kilgore Road
Kalamazoo, MI 49001-5598

American Dog Breeders Assn.
P.O. Box 1771
Salt Lake City, UT 84110
(Registers American Pit Bull Terriers)

Canadian Kennel Club
89 Skyway Avenue
Etobicoke, Ontario
Canada M9W 6R4

National Stock Dog Registry
P.O. Box 402
Butler, IN 46721
(Registers working stock dogs)

Orthopedic Foundation for Animals (OFA)
2300 E. Nifong Blvd.
Columbia, MO 65201-3856
(Hip registry)

Activity Clubs

Write to these organizations for information on the
activities they sponsor.

American Kennel Club
51 Madison Avenue
New York, NY 10010
(Conformation Shows, Obedience Trials, Field
Trials and Hunting Tests, Agility, Canine Good

Citizen, Lure Coursing, Herding, Tracking,
Earthdog Tests, Coonhunting.)

United Kennel Club
100 E. Kilgore Road
Kalamazoo, MI 49001-5598
(Conformation Shows, Obedience Trials, Agility,
Hunting for Various Breeds, Terrier Trials and
more.)

North American Flyball Assn.
1342 Jeff St.
Ypsilanti, MI 48198

International Sled Dog Racing Assn.
P.O. Box 446
Norman, ID 83848-0446

North American Working Dog Assn., Inc.
Southeast Kreisgruppe
P.O. Box 833
Brunswick, GA 31521

Trainers

Association of Pet Dog Trainers
P.O. Box 385
Davis, CA 95617
(800) PET–DOGS

American Dog Trainers' Network
161 West 4th St.
New York, NY 10014
(212) 727–7257

**National Association of Dog Obedience
Instructors**
2286 East Steel Rd.
St. Johns, MI 48879

Associations

American Dog Owners Assn.
1654 Columbia Tpk.
Castleton, NY 12033
(Combats anti-dog legislation)

Delta Society
P.O. Box 1080
Renton, WA 98057-1080
(Promotes the human/animal bond through
pet-assisted therapy and other programs)

Dog Writers Assn. of America (DWAA)
Sally Cooper, Secy.
222 Woodchuck Ln.
Harwinton, CT 06791

National Assn. for Search and Rescue (NASAR)
P.O. Box 3709
Fairfax, VA 22038

Therapy Dogs International
6 Hilltop Road
Mendham, NJ 07945